PERSONAL

HISTORIES

New Atlantic Media
Chapel Hill, NC
2021

PERSONAL HISTORIES

Peter Filene

Personal Histories. Copyright © 2021 by Peter Filene
All Rights Reserved.

All Photographs:
Copyright © 2021 by Peter Filene
All Rights Reserved.

Book Design by Tim Hubbard
New Atlantic Media
Chapel Hill, NC

10 9 8 7 6 5 4 3 2 1
ISBN 978-1-7375336-0-3

Printed in the United States of America

Also By PETER FILENE

Striving Fathers, Troubled Sons: From John Adams to James Baldwin

The Joy of Teaching: A Practical Guide for New College Instructors

Him/Her/Self: Gender Identities in Modern America

In the Arms of Others: A Cultural History of the Right to Die

Home and Away (a novel)

Men in the Middle: Work and Family in the Lives of Middle-Aged Men

Americans and the Soviet Experiment, 1917-1933

CONTENTS

	Preface	1
Chapter 1	Living through Books and War	5
Chapter 2	Recollecting My Father	15
Chapter 3	The Spiero Sisters	45
Chapter 4	Marriage and Memory	91
Chapter 5	Harvard Days	103
Chapter 6	Reckless Days	125
Chapter 7	A Letter to my Students	159
Chapter 8	The Cure for Love	193
Chapter 9	The Art of Lost and Found	203
Chapter 10	Quarantining with Heidegger	213

List of Photographs

Peter and Robert Filene, 1947 .... *10*
Finkelstein family, 1927 .... *23*
Herman Filene, 1933 .... *24*
Herman Filene, 1952 .... *29*
Ursula Spiero, 1930 .... *31*
Herman Filene's letter, 1938 .... *39*
Herman, Peter and Robert Filene, 1950 .... *43*
Spiero house, Hamburg *46*
Christiane, Olga and Ursula Spiero, 1927 .... *54*
Ursula Spiero, 1930 .... *56*
Josi and Fritz Einstein, 1920s *59*
Christina Ilisch, 1930 .... *60*
Max and Christina Warburg, 1941 .... *65*
Josi Warburg, 1950 .... *69*
Sabine Gova, 1957 .... *72*
Sabine Gova's letter, 1993 .... *77*
Peter, Bob and Ursula Filene, c. 1954 .... *79*
Ursula Filene's letter, 1962 .... *81*
Ursula Filene, early 1960s *82*
Peter Filene, newspaper photo, 1963 .... *116*
Lincoln University seal *127*
Benjamin and Jeanette Filene, 1966 .... *139*
Benjamin and Peter Filene, 1966 .... *141*
Project Hinton poster, 1969 .... *178*
Paris Façade, double exposure, 1994 .... *206*
Smoking in the Tuileries, double exposure, 2003 .... *207*
Blues If You Want, photocollage, 2019 .... *210*

Preface

As a historian, I constructed pieces of strangers' past into a coherent interpretation. As the historian of my own past, I discovered that memoir is a trickier process. In the course of sixty-plus years, I had filled several large boxes with my journals, letters and photographs. When I dived into this evidence, I was surprised by how much I had forgotten: activities, acquaintances, my ideas and reactions. But there's forgetting and there's misremembering. I was dumfounded to find I had unwittingly reconstructed crucial past events into new stories. Ultimately, this memoir explores the ambiguities of not only what I have done, but of who I thought I was.

These ten essays form a collage. They follow me from birth to middle age, leap silently across thirty years, and conclude with finding love and meaning in the time of Covid. Most of them focus on me, but my father takes center stage in one essay, my mother and her three sisters in another. Two essays explore the neurology of memory and the sense of direction. What, then, holds these pieces together?

Teaching. That's the obvious answer. I found myself writing with passion and confidence, sometimes lyrically, as I recounted my experiences in the college classroom. Teaching, my lifelong calling, runs throughout the book.

It's crosscut by a second theme, another layer of the collage: *learning*. Even as I learned to teach better, I developed skills far beyond the classroom: civil rights work in the 1960s; writing fiction in the 80s; and since then, fine-art photography. And I was engaged in a kind of learning closer to my sense of self. In the very process of writing these pages, I saw familiar features of my life in a new light. My father, for example. The memoir was teaching me.

Finally, and most disconcerting, there is *unlearning*. As I turned the yellowing pages of my letters and journal, I had to dismantle some basic certainties I'd lived by. My perilous fantasy of Paris, for example; and how I proposed marriage. While confronting this intensely personal history, I experienced surges of emotion: pleasure, wistfulness, regret, shame.

In the end, here I am, collected in ten essays that form a multilayered self-portrait.

***

I asked my parents too late about their lives before I was born. When they died at sixty and seventy-two, I had only a precious ninety-minute taped interview with my father. Mindful of that loss, I've published this book for my grandchildren if and when they become curious about their Opa.

I'm indebted to my Thursday-afternoon writing group—Laurel Goldman, Angela Davis-Gardner, Joe Burgo, Christina Askounis and Peggy Payne—for invaluable critiques and long friendship. From start to finish, you inspired this project.

Preface

Frank Einstein and Christina Mills made important corrections.

I'm grateful beyond words for the love and support from my wonderful family: Benjamin Filene and Rachel Seidman, Becky Broun and Michael Durbin, Bob and Sue Filene, and Jeanette Pfaff.

Thank you, Stuart Macdonald, for everything.

Personal Histories

Chapter 1

Living through Books and War

I was born reading. Which is to say, I don't remember a time when I couldn't read. And also to say I've lived a large part of my life, often the most exciting part, inside books. I still recall the grand thump inside my chest, age five or so, as I stood at the desk in the Children's Section of the New York Public Library and printed my name on the membership card. "He's unusually young," the librarian said over my head to my mother. "Yes," Mommy replied. "He started reading early."

So I recall. Memory, we know, is untrustworthy. But I happen to have the kind of evidence a memoirist craves. It rests inside a leather-bound book, elaborately embossed around the edges, which my mother's grandfather Joseph Spiero has dedicated, with a handsome flourish of calligraphy, to his "beloved and ever dear" fiancée Ida in 1873 in Konigsberg, Germany. During the next six decades, the loosely sewn gilt-edged pages remain blank, until April 8, 1940, three months after my birth in Manhattan. "Mein Liebling," my mother addresses me in the first of scores of letters that soon shift from German to English and end in May 1944 with an eleven-page typed letter to "My Darling."

Sure enough, there I am on page eight, dashing into my childhood of books. "You start learning the ABC and can read letters, not words, since before Christmas [1943]. You try to teach Bobby [my two-year-old brother] things you learn in school." Every Saturday morning, I would tuck the library card in my pocket and ride up Forty-Second Street on the trolley clang-clanging at every traffic light to Fifth Avenue, climb the stairs between the magnificent stone lions, and after long deliberation, select four books (the limit) to take home.

But my story also took place in the world outside of books. I was born in the midst of a war. It not only killed millions of people in Europe and Asia. It invaded the New York Public Library, it shadowed my family, and in ways I recognized only years later, it shaped my career. When memoir joins hands with history, the plotline thickens.

***

From 1942 to 1945 the Library published annual reports in hand-sized pamphlets, five by seven inches, one or two dozen pages, with playful titles on the cover: *Lucky Books*, *Busy Books* and *Books Alive*. Open them, however, and one finds grim news. "Fourteen lean years have all but wrecked the Circulation Department. Many of its branch buildings are obsolete, all are in need of renovation and repair, its book stock is a battered wreck, its staff depleted." The situation was "a disgrace to the City, a source of shame to the librarians...." Nevertheless, we can't "subscribe to hopeless, shallow pessimism." "Hard luck? Maybe. But neither you nor the

Library is griping about it. There is a war on and the thing to do is to win it."¹

On the long road toward victory, the library busily served the needs of New Yorkers. "Beset by rationing, shortages of materials and labor, disappearing cooks, crowds and high prices," people wanted how-to books. Against "the insistent clamor of the radio, the newsreel and the headline," people were reading religion, philosophy and sociology. Reference librarians were helping scholars who were in exile from Europe. "How great the physical destruction or equally damaging looting of European libraries will be no one can say. "²

The destruction would be worse than they imagined. In Berlin, on the evening of May 10, 1933, Nazi students invaded public libraries and private homes, threw 25,000 "unGerman" books onto the street, and burned them in a massive bonfire on Franz Josef Platz. Joseph Goebbels, the Reich Minister of Propaganda, congratulated the mob. "The era of extreme Jewish intellectualism is now at an end. The future German man will not just be a man of books, but a man of character. And thus you do well in this midnight hour to commit the evil spirit of the past to the flames." During the next twelve years, approximately one hundred million books burned.³ What the Nazis began, Allied bombers in 1943-45 supplemented with air raids that rained bombs and fire on cities across Germany. One of those raids destroyed the Berlin apartment that housed ten to twenty thousand books owned by Heinrich Spiero, who was the nationally renowned historian of German literature and also my grandfather.

***

PERSONAL HISTORIES

My mother emigrated to New York in 1936, where she met and married my father, also a German refugee. They were safe but her parents were increasingly imperiled as the Nazis began deporting Jews to Poland and preparing for war. Desperately, my mother tried to secure a job and a visa for her parents. In 1938 the University of Delaware invited Spiero to teach. But he was reluctant to leave his "*Heimat*," albeit a homeland where the Nazis prohibited him, a descendant of Jews, from teaching and writing. Meanwhile, illness and German bureaucracy added more obstacles. By 1941, it was too late. America was at war and she lost contact. "We know that my parents did not have to go [to Poland]," she wrote in the journal. "We don't know where they are and whether they are still alive. Every other member of your father's and my family has been deported, even the 80 year old sister of your great grandfather Spiero."

As she endured this fearful silence, she wrote to me, her newborn son. "One day you will learn … about Refugees and bombardments, about black-outs and air-shelters. Let us hope that you have only to learn about it." As a historian, I would indeed learn all about the horrors of World War II. But in the course of writing this memoir, I discovered a surprise. As a child, I knew more than either she or I realized.

According to psychologists, young children can remember events before the age of three. With 50 percent accuracy, they recall two weeks afterwards the sequence of their actions as well as the objects they used to produce that sequence. They remember emotions, places and events. But amnesia soon sets in. After the age of seven, the memories begin to fade and by the time of adolescence, they are lost. A cumulative story of self-identity, filtered through cultural models, takes over.[4] Now at the age of seventy-nine, in a written counterpoint with my mother's sentences, I can fill in some of the gaps of the story.

I made sense of things, first of all, through spoken words. I was mostly silent until, at the age of two, I began speaking in sentences. Bilingual sentences. Amid the war, my parents didn't speak German in public and didn't teach me German, for fear I would speak it on the street or in the park. Still, "Daddy and I speak German at home and we know you understand quite a bit. You lately started repeating certain sentences and you speak with quite an accent." In turn, across all the decades, I can hear her non-English cadences and inflections.

As the first-born, I spied hungrily on the world of grownups. And as a bilingual spy, I acquired information larger than child-sized. Rationing, for example. Everything from sugar to baseballs was doled out in tightfisted portions, and I understood why. "The war does not mean much to you," Mommy wrote when I was four, "only sometimes when you want something and don't get it, you yourself say 'There is a war going on.'" My awareness extended even further afield, beyond the circle of my wants and my family. "You heard our new maid talk about her husband, who is overseas with the Army[,] and you asked 'When will the war be over, so that the people can come back?' But I know you don't understand the meaning of it all." My father stayed home. Given his disability from polio, his military service consisted of standing on the roof at night as an air raid warden, watching for German bombers. He was safe. Until the war was over, though, my mother wouldn't know whether her father was alive or dead.

***

Peter and Robert Filene, 1947

Heinrich Spiero was born in Konigsberg in 1876.[5] As the firstborn child and only son of a prosperous Jewish family, he was destined for success. The only question was which field he would choose. At the age of eighteen, like many German Jews seeking to assimilate, he was baptized as a Lutheran. After graduating university (Philosophy, History, Art History) and studying law, he worked as a manager in his father's shipping firm. But business didn't hold his interest. After marrying Olga Jolowicz (also Lutheran) in 1900, he moved to an artistic neighborhood of Hamburg, where he became involved in cultural and literary circles, founded an art society, and—as their guest book documents—he and Olga hosted lively gatherings of artists and illustrious public figures. Between 1901 and 1911, four daughters were born, including my mother Ursula. According to Sabine, the oldest girl, Heinrich was "friendly—though never affectionate." His study was off-limits to the children. But on Sunday afternoons, immaculately dressed as always in velvet coat with hat and cane, he led them on daylong "excursions" around Hamburg, teaching about architecture and history.[6] Meanwhile, he somehow managed to write an astonishing number of books—histories, novels, and poetry—thirty in all. After the First World War, the family moved to a twelve-room apartment in Berlin, the cultural capital, with a staff of five or six servants. He proceeded to write another forty books and edited the ten-volume *Jedermann Lexicon (Everyman's Encyclopedia)*.

In 1933, everything changed. Hitler's policies began relentlessly stripping Jews of their rights, their professions and property, and finally their lives. Spiero was forbidden to write or teach. Because he was in a *"privilegierten Mischehe"* (mixed marriage) with Olga, he was spared deportation to a concentration camp. But his status as a Christian Jew was precarious. The slightest violation of anti-Semitic regulations could jeopardize him. Still, for three years he led the Paulus-Bund, an organization that provided aid to "non-Aryan Christians," education for children evicted from public schools, and legal advice and charity for adults. But Jews, even partial Jews, faced an increasingly narrow existence: yellow stars; designated shops; curfews. By 1941, 74,000 Jews in Berlin were thrown out of their homes. The Spieros went from a four-room apartment to a one-room apt in a *Judenhaus* on Victoria-Luise-Platz.

In November 1943, an Allied air raid bombed the house. "While Father and I stood outside," Olga recalled, "all around us a sea of flames fell from the fire storm, with sparks falling on our belongings, coats and hats, and we saw how the fire ate what was left in our house. Suddenly Father disappeared; I couldn't believe that he had been thrown sideways into the bushes. But eventually there came Father serenely [*seelenruhig*] out a door we no longer used, out of the burning stairway where the floorboards were still burning, the elevator was scorched and lay underneath, burning of course, and he had two books in his hands. Our guestbook [of illustrious acquaintances in Hamburg] and *Amerika-Briefe* [letters from their visit to America]. 'I wanted, [he said], to rescue these two souvenirs of a better time.'"[7]

They survived the war, boarding with their daughter's family, but faced a desperate future. Shelter, food, income, health: everything was in ruins. My nine-year-old cousin went out at night to steal potatoes from Allied freight trains. Six-foot-tall Spiero weighed 100 pounds. In the spring of 1946, dictating to a secretary, he began his last book, *Geschichte des Deutschen Romans* [The History of the German Novel]. Since his own library was destroyed, he consulted the books of friends, but primarily he relied on memory. By December he had completed the 550-page book. When Olga later copyedited the manuscript and wrote the index and footnotes, she found he had recalled every citation correctly.

During the exceptionally cold winter, Spiero became fatally ill with pneumonia. My mother frantically applied to the State Department for a passport, but before she could make her way through the red tape, he died in March 1947.[8]

***

After V-E Day, my mother made up for the wartime silence with a torrent of words. Sitting at her desk in the living room, she typed multi-paged, single-spaced letters recounting news of our daily lives and asking questions about her parents and relatives in Europe. At night I fell asleep to the staccato of her typewriter keys.

In high school, I wrote a short story about George Washington's troops at Valley Forge. Why this historical episode, I have no idea. It wasn't exactly appropriate for a Quaker school, and I don't recall doing any research, but the five-page story was published in *The Stove*, our school literary magazine. My first publication! I couldn't stop gazing at my words set with such formality on the page.

 One evening shortly afterwards, I was standing behind her as she typed, watching the words chase to the righthand margin and go "bing," again and again, as she narrated what Bobby and I had done the past week, what she was reading, whom she had lunched with, the weather—a homely saga. "You should write an autobiography, or a family history," I said. "The four sisters, the Nazis and the war: it would be great."

She stopped typing, turned to look at me. "No, darling, that's not something I can do. You're the real writer."

I heard it not simply as praise. I heard it as a confederacy between us. But now I recognize there was more at work. I feel a bond between me and Heinrich Spiero, the man of letters, author of seventy books, owner of a library of twenty thousand books that turned to ash when I was three years old.

My mother died in 1967, age sixty, a few months before my first book was published.

Personal Histories

1. *Books Again, 1945* (New York: The NYPL, 1946), 7; *Busy Books: The New York Public Library in 1944* (New York: The NYPL, 1945), 22-23; *Lucky Books: The New York Public Library in 1942* (New York: The NYPL, 1943), 15-16, 9.
2. *Busy Books*, 22-23
3. Matthew Battles, *Library* (New York: Norton, 2003), 164, 167—citing Louis P Lochner, in *Nazism, 1919-1945: A Documentary Reader*, ed. J. Noakes and G. Pridham (Exeter, 1983). OR Lochner in *The Goebbels Diaries, 1942-1943*.
4. Rebecca Rupp, *Committed to Memory: How We Remember and Why We Forget* (New York: Crown, 1998), 215-25; Paptricia J. Bauer, "Oh Where, Oh Where Have Those Early Memories Gone? A Developmental Perspective," *Psychological Science Agenda* (December 2004); Gail S. Goodman and Annika Melinder, "The Development of Autobiographical Memory: A New Model," in *Everyday Memory*, ed. Svein Magnussen and Tore Hestrup (New York: Psychology Press, 2008), 111-34; Qi Wang and Martin A. Conway, "Autobiographical Memory, Self, and Culture," in *Memory and Society: Psychological Perspectives*, ed. Lars-Goran Nilsson and Nobuo Ohta (New York: Psychology Press, 2006), 9-27.
5. For most of the biographical information, I have gratefully relied on Anna Rohr, *Dr. Heinrich Spiero (1876-1947): Sein Wirken fur die Christen Judischer Herkunft under dem NS-Regime* (Berlin: Metropol, 2015).
6. Sabine Gova to Peter Filene, March 1986.
7. Olga to her children, Nov. 28, 1943, quoted in Rohr, *Heinrich Spiero*, 105. My translation.
8. My interview with granddaughters Karola Buerkner and Dotti Seeliger, April 2012; Sabine Gova to Peter Filene, March 1986; and for passport application, copies of letters in my possession.

Chapter 2

RECOLLECTING MY FATHER

Personal Histories

It's late in the game to be trying to know him better. At age seventy-six I'm in the eighth inning, or maybe the ninth. (Baseball was, to my dismay, one of those American things he never understood. The "World Serious," he would say in his German accent.) He's been gone almost half my life, and my mother and their friends even longer. Vital details are buried. Family stories have worn thin, like shirts that used to be a particular color. My past is filling up with absences.

And when I resort to my memories, I run up against his silences. Of course he talked, we talked, but not about his past. Supposedly there once was a boy playing in Berlin streets, a youth skiing without a limp and a cane, a *Rechtsanwalt* with a Doctorate of Jurisprudence before Hitler disbarred Jewish lawyers. Yet he cloaked these selves behind stolid silence.

As for the present, he had more to say about politics or my schoolwork than about his emotions.

Why bother, then, to try to recollect him? Let the dead rest in peace, you might reasonably advise. Life is not measured out in innings, you point out. I agree, and yet, for some reason, I want to, need to, tell his story. Perhaps because I'm a retired historian who is tired of writing about the histories of strangers. Certainly because I want to fill in the gap for my children, who barely remember their "Grandfather," and for my grandchildren, who know only his face in the photo album.

∗∗∗

There was, to begin with, the matter of his names.

Herman. Actually, back in Germany it had been spelled

with two n's. "Hare-mahn," that's how my parents and their refugee friends pronounced it.

L. It stands for nothing. L as in "Nothing"? No, nothing, just the letter L, all by its lonesome, because he thought Americans expect to see something between one's first and last names.

Filene. Which seems Italian (pronounced "Fee-layna") or French ("Fee-len"), not German, so that stirs up a small mystery until I explain that he arrived in the United States as Finkelstein. "That was too European," he explained to me. In other words, too Jewish. Yes, ironic, isn't it? The impoverished refugee from Nazi Germany turns into Herman L. Filene ("Fi-leen"), adopting the name of the wealthy Boston department store owner.

***

He arrived in 1933 with 250 words of English. I wish I had asked him which words. *Grocery store? Soap? Blanket? Newspaper? Tomorrow and yesterday? Subway? Alarm clock?* One needs an army of nouns to navigate a foreign city in the dead of winter in the depths of the Depression.

The only word he mentioned, with a rueful laugh, was "Tare-mo-mayter," because again and again nobody understood him, until finally a savvy druggist unraveled his pronunciation and handed him a thermometer.

Was he ill? Or taking precautions? After having been shoved out of his profession and his homeland, a man might want to arm himself at least against germs.

And what about adjectives? *Lonely? Frightened? Sad?* I

doubt my father packed such words among his precious 250. After all, I rarely heard them while I was growing up. He was a man who dealt with practicalities, and feelings were impractical. On the day after Christmas, two days after his arrival, he was walking on Fifth Avenue and "I almost cried," he told me. But as I was filling up with empathic grief, he said: "there was such a wind and cold."

He expressed himself in objects.

There was his father's gold pocket watch. He would open the lid, hold it against my ear, and as if from across the Atlantic Ocean, I heard a frail chime, one, two, three, holding my breath until twelve and a tremulous silence.

There was the heavy, dark wooden savings bank that he set on the table—as big as a bread box but more mysterious. I tugged on the little drawer that slid out like a tongue, laid my penny in the indentation, and pushed. The coin fell inside with a soft clunk, buried forever. Once he showed me the trick to open the bank, but I've forgotten it.

There was the burgundy satin robe he secretly bought at Lord and Taylor. On my mother's birthday, or maybe it was their anniversary, he combined plywood and curtain rods into a five-foot-tall rectangle on which he hung the robe. "You can come in now," he called to her, opening the living room door. "*Aber Du*," she exclaimed in a voice full of love.

He sat in watchful silence, the paterfamilias, while others spoke for him.

His sister, Dorothy: "Oh, Peter, if only you had known your father before. He won't talk about it, but I tell you, he was so happy."

My mother: During those Sunday afternoon long-distance phone calls when I was at college, she would ask "how are you feeling? what are you doing?" and report the family news, while I heard him breathing on the extension phone.

My stepmother: On the morning of his funeral service, she insisted he had believed in God, although I had never heard him utter anything more theological than "thank God it was only a flat tire."

***

Elevators have a strange habit of showing up in these pages.

Shortly after my father arrived in America, a rich banker remarked: "Be an elevator boy. Fastest way to get up in this country."

"It was very facetious," he recalled forty years later. "I didn't like that at all." Even if he'd had more money and more English, he couldn't resume his career in a system governed by Anglo Saxon rather than Germanic law. But the ex-*Rechtsanwalt* with a Doctorate of Jurisprudence was no elevator boy. He was determined to climb, stair by stair, into the middle class.

When he was disbarred, he at first considered driving his father's Buick from Berlin to Palestine and starting over as a taxi driver. But crossing the Near East seemed too dangerous.

So he crossed the Atlantic instead. There might have been an opening in a bank or department store or, God forbid, elevator. But by chance, he ended up selling life insurance. Through his cousin he met a salesman at a fair in Leipzig who knew three businessmen in the States, one of whom was the brother-in-law of Mr. Fried, who worked in the New England

Mutual Life Insurance Company branch in Manhattan. "This is a hopeless case," Mr. Fried said at the end of the interview, "but I want to do a good deed." Although my father knew nothing about life insurance, he took the job "on a hunch." His first case netted $180.

Determination, chance and hunch thrust him happenstance into the future. Life insurance fit him like a three-piece suit. As a man of misfortunes, with one more to come, he was determined—dare we say destined?—to protect others against the dark turns of life.

Still, he didn't give up on the career Hitler had snatched from him. At breakfast he would look at me over *The New York Times* and explain in a reverent tone what the Supreme Court had decided yesterday. Holmes, Brandeis ("the first Jew on the Court, you know"), Warren: these were names as holy to him as DiMaggio, Mantle and Rizzuto to me. He wanted me to go to law school, Harvard Law School, to be exact, and eventually sit where Brandeis had sat. Maybe he didn't say that, but I thought I knew what he had in mind. Or maybe that's what I thought I owed him. The best I could do, though, was Harvard graduate school in history. During one of his visits to Cambridge, I took him into the lobby of Langdell Hall, where we gazed at the portraits of Holmes, Brandeis ("the first Jew on the Court, you know") and the other saints of jurisprudence.

***

"I got sick" is the way he put it. On a July afternoon in 1935, an ambulance team arrived at his apartment on Third Avenue and 46th St., walked up five flights of stairs, loaded him—six-foot-tall, 180 pounds—onto the stretcher and carried him down (or did they abandon the stretcher and carry his body?) to the waiting ambulance. Then (with siren wailing?) they sped to the hospital and the emergency room and the iron lung.

Infantile poliomyelitis, as the name announces, almost always afflicts children, but my father was twenty-nine. He was one of approximately seven thousand new cases in the United States. Two years after he fled Germany, he once again belonged to a victimized minority—a minority of the minority, in fact. But this time he couldn't emigrate.

The iron lung was invented by two Harvard physicians in 1927. It performed the breathing for patients whose chest muscles were paralyzed by the polio virus. It was an eight-foot-long, rectangular, metal box, powered by an electric motor that controlled the air pressure inside, pulling air in and out of the lungs. The patient lay on a bed (or "cookie tray," some called it) that slid in and out, his head protruding at one end, looking up into a mirror at a narrow reflection of the room. Nurses reached in through portal windows to adjust limbs or sheets or hot packs. In hospital wards throughout the nation, iron lungs were lined up side by side like coffins in a warehouse encasing human beings like my father.

"I got sick," he told me, and I was too respectful, and also too frightened, to ask for details. Those months in the hospital are the Dark Ages of this history. I heard recollections by my aunt Dorothy, but given her inclination to melancholy, we have to take them with a few grains of salt.

He lay in the iron lung for some time—a week? two weeks? I don't know—and in any case, time for my father was fifteen inhalations and exhalations a minute, the squeeze and release of the machine. After some time the doctors slid him out and told him he would live. Unfortunately, though, he would never walk again. That's what they also told him.

The next part I borrow from other people's memoirs and scholarly histories of medicine. Every day they wrapped his shriveled legs in hot blankets that hurt like hell and had a wet, wooly smell one never forgets. They massaged the muscles. They pummeled and twisted and stretched him . He pulled himself to a sitting position, lifted weights, endowed his shoulders and chest with the power he had lost in his legs.

Every day or two, after Dorothy finished her shift unpacking boxes in a department store, she made the long subway ride uptown to visit her brother. Then she took the subway downtown to their apartment and studied for her courses at Columbia School of Social Work. Eventually she rented an apartment for them on Sixth Avenue and 46th Street, this one with an elevator.

He entered the hospital in July. In April he walked out on crutches. Soon he would limp with a cane.

"Let me assert my firm belief that the only thing we have to fear is fear itself," Roosevelt proclaimed, "nameless, unreasoning, unjustified terror which paralyzes needed efforts to convert retreat into advance."

"If only you had known your father as he used to be," Dorothy frequently lamented to me, "skiing, laughing, full of life!" She sounded like someone who had lost a lover. Which in a way she was. She had followed her older brother to the United States, changed her last name when he changed his, shared his apartment with him, visited him day after day in the hospital, and shared the second apartment. In 1938, however, my father married my mother and moved to an apartment downstairs. Without Dorothy! She couldn't believe it. For the rest of her never-married life she and my mother exchanged barely disguised resentment.

But the question remains: when did my father become the stoical person I grew up with? With emigration, when Finkelstein became Filene? After polio, when ski poles became crutches? Or did Dorothy, the lonely sister, ignore the silence and stoicism that were there all along? According to his memory, for example, he skied only twice in his life.

On the other hand, there's a 1927 photo of the Finkelstein family posing with their sporty automobile, Herr und Frau standing beside the rear door, Dorothea perched on the hood with lots of leg showing, and Hermann in the driver's seat.

Finkelstein family, 1927

And look at him standing on board the ship to America, pipe in hand, jaunty.

Herman Filene, 1933

And he would flirt. My brother remembers taking a high school girl friend to the New England Mutual office twenty-seven floors above Fifth Avenue, the paternal castle. Our father bestowed questions and jokes upon the girl in a voice warmer and more musical than we were used to. I overheard that same voice one afternoon when he was talking on the phone with a long-distance operator.

How can I reconcile the tight-lipped father who limped away from the iron lung with the father who was the life of the party?

***

My parents were born in the same year, 1906, and after the Great War they lived in the same city, Berlin, but they would meet in New York City in 1938. I wonder whether they ever strolled past each other on Unter den Linden or sat together on a streetcar to the Tiergarten. Better yet, my fantasy alights on that Berlin restaurant my mother described with a mischievous smile, the one with a telephone on every table. "When you were attracted to someone eating alone across the room," she said, "you could give him a ring." What if that had been my handsome father across the room?

"There is something quite searching and wonderful about seeing much of history as a chaos of chance," the historian Jill Lepore remarks. "It has a few pitfalls, however." On the one hand, it obscures how people in power—Nazis, for example, and Roosevelt—determine events, and how impersonal forces such as technology and the economy do the same. On the other hand, it obscures how individuals shape and steer their course though life.

How might I tell my father's story giving credit to forces, choices and chance? Try this.

The Nazis befell him and he escaped to safety. Then the Great Depression and polio befell him and he fought back to stand on his feet. Then one enchanted evening across a crowded room, Ursula Spiero befell him. It was March of 1938, at a party of his longtime friend Hank. "Nice to have met you," Herman said to her at the end of the evening. "I'm taking my sister home." But that casual goodbye was the start of an urgent romance. By October they married. I was born in January 1940, followed two years later by my brother Bobby.

It's hard to maintain the balance between "had-to-end-up-there" and "might-have-gone-otherwise." As Lepore says, "All biography is teleological to one degree or another, which is a problem, but a knowable one."[1]

I know, and it's especially problematic when the biographer is writing about his parents with himself as the outcome.

***

I was five years old, returning with my mother from an errand on a chilly April afternoon in 1945. As we stepped into the elevator of our apartment building, Frank, the chubby, affable elevator man, said something to her and she burst into tears. Mommy was crying! In public!

"What's wrong?" I asked.

She squeezed my hand. "The President has died."

I don't know how my father reacted to the news. Probably with lips pulled back tight, eyes narrowed, perhaps some muttered phrase in German before retreating into silence. That was how he would deal with other calamities: the death of his doctor friend, Kurt; the fracture of his right kneecap; my divorce.

Franklin D. Roosevelt had reigned over our family like a god. . . with Hitler as the devil. FDR was in the White House working to take Americans out of bread lines when my father stepped off the boat in Manhattan with a useless law degree and a $1,000 loan from his cousin. Roosevelt was holding on to a lectern with ten-pound steel braces on his legs, announcing the Social Security program when my father lay inside the iron lung. Roosevelt was re-elected by 58 percent when my father walked into his office on Forty-second Street, where I picture the other life insurance salesmen and the secretaries greeting him with cheers.

"Tell your students about the fireside chats," Father urged me years later in an ardent voice. "Every week or so, Peter, the President talked on the radio about his policies just as if he was sitting there in my living room." By then, having taught my course on "Recent U.S. History" several times, I knew otherwise. The fact is, FDR delivered an average of only two fireside chats per year. But why would I step between my father and his beloved president with my scholarly corrections? Even if I had persuaded him that he had spent no more than twenty-three evenings sitting by the radio in his living room, listening to that melodious, aristocratic voice, his affection for Roosevelt wouldn't have wavered in the slightest. As I liked to remind my students, there's history and there's the past, and they don't always coincide. What we remember has its own life, its own truth.

Indeed, measuring the impact of those fireside chats, my father was correct. Consider this piece of evidence. On the evening of May 27, 1941, when war was raging in Europe and the Pacific, electric meters in power stations across the United States suddenly jumped. People were turning on their radios—sixty-five million people in twenty million homes, 70 percent of the total home audience. President Roosevelt was about to deliver a fireside chat explaining his plans for national defense. Only one other broadcast had rivaled this popularity: the second Joe Louis-Max Schmeling world heavyweight championship boxing match in 1938. On his best nights, Jack Benny won half as many listeners as the President.

I bet my father was one of those sixty-five million, heartened to hear Roosevelt defy the isolationists and warn, "it would be suicide to wait until the Nazis are in our front yard." The Brown Bomber defeated German-born Schmeling in the first round. Roosevelt would need almost four years, and died a month before V-E Day.

***

When my father was sitting, he could lift his left leg only by hoisting it with both hands, so driving a standard shift car was out of the question. Roosevelt acquired a specially built Ford Phaeton operated entirely by hand levers, but Herman Filene wasn't a Roosevelt. He traveled to and from his office on the trolley. (I doubt he could afford a taxi.) If he made a Sunday excursion beyond the city, he bought a ticket on a Short Line bus or the Long Island Railroad. The youth who had contemplated escaping the Nazis by driving from Berlin to Palestine was in the hands of strangers.

In 1945, all that seemed about to change. Oldsmobile announced production of an eight-cylinder sedan equipped with four-speed, fully automatic transmission. Hydramatic!

Herman rushed to the nearest Oldsmobile dealer and paid a $100 deposit. A year went by, two years, no car. "Finally," he recalled, "I phoned the vice president of General Motors and told them my story." Stoic survivor that he was, I assume this was no sob story, just the hard facts, presented with the same trustworthy calm as his discussions with life insurance clients. Sure enough, "the next day I got a call. Be at the lot on Eleventh Avenue." He paid $1,800 to the cashier, the motor was running, "and off I went." Well, not quite. Since he had no license, a friend did the driving. Soon, though, he joined his fellow Americans who had waited through four years of rationed gas and tires until they could sit behind the wheel again, commuting to work, taking the wife and kids on vacation with overnight lodging at a motel cabin, on the road. See the U.S.A. in your Chevrolet.

Daddy loved driving fast, up the Merritt Parkway, left arm on the window ledge, cigarette smoke trailing through the

Herman Filene, 1952

little triangular window. Mommy sat beside him, chatting and smoking, enjoying the classical music on the radio. For years he refused to let her drive, even to get a license. Her job was to offer him Life Savers, referee border wars between me and my brother in the back seat, and twist around to spot any police cars that might be stealing up behind us as he exceeded the speed limit. "Nah, Hermann," she would mutter when he honked at a too-slow car ahead or passed across a solid line.

Decades later, while writing a book about the history of gender identities, I learned the conceptual language to label what was going on. But even as a kid in the back seat, I understood that Hydramatic gave my father the power to reclaim a part of his pre-polio manhood.

The counterpart for my mother was her IBM Selectric typewriter. At sixty words per minute she poured out her own frustrations.

Ursula came from the illustrious Spiero family in Hamburg and then Berlin. It wasn't easy growing up wedged third behind an intellectually ambitious older sister and a tomboy, and ahead of a charming youngest sister, all of them seeking the attention of a famous father secluded among 16,000 books in his study writing, writing, writing, and a mother devoted primarily to him. Usu had a lively intelligence, plus a potent blend of hot temper and dark-eyed beauty.

✳✳✳

As a teenager, she joined the *Wandervögel* (Wandering Birds), a youth group who spent idyllic weekends in nature, camping in fields, cooking meals over campfires, and singing folk songs. She eventually earned a nursing degree, while

Ursula Spiero, 1930

enjoying the irreverent pleasures of Weimar Berlin nightclubs and theater. Three years after the Nazis took power, Ursula emigrated to New York and found work in a doctor's office. Two years later, she married Herman, settled down in their two-bedroom apartment, and in short order had two sons.

"We decided it was better for you," my father explained to me years afterwards, "that she stop work and stay home." Bobby and I kept her busy. So did housekeeping and meals. And so did the *Abrechnung*, the monthly budget. Herman gave her an allowance, out of which she had to record every purchase. August 1942: 93¢ laundry; 25¢ stamps; 46¢ cigarettes; 10¢ sugar; $1.10 shoes—food, drugs, carfare, gifts—$138 received,

$121.63 spent. She disliked the chore. Some months she jiggered the numbers to balance the *Abrechnung*.

Still, she had energy to spare. After the war she carried bulky packages, thousands of them, to the post office for her family in Europe: cans of tomatoes, beans, tuna fish; shirts, jackets, gloves, socks; Aspirin and vitamins; the *Reader's Digest*; paper on which her father could finally write the book he had kept in his mind during four years without paper. She phoned and lunched with myriads of friends and acquaintances, invited them to dinner, and attended their parties. She crocheted scarves, caps and blankets for relatives, friends, even the butcher's newborn child. She read the latest novels. She redesigned the living room with Danish furniture. She won a *Daily News* contest for the best apple pie recipe. She attended concerts at Carnegie Hall.

And always she wrote letters. Lying in bed at night I heard her electric typewriter's eager clickety-clack like the staccato of Ginger Rogers tap dancing. She wrote to her mother in Berlin, her sister and aunt in London, her cousin in California, and who knows how many friends and acquaintances dispersed by Hitler around the globe. Multipage, single-space letters stretching margin to margin with news about the family, the weather, what she was reading, whom she had met, how she was feeling.

***

Stop! This is a memoir about my father, yet here he's been overshadowed when my mother enters the room. It's like when I was growing up. She talked and he observed. And more than I care to remember, I took sides. Her side.

"Daddy and I are wondering," she said one afternoon, "why you never considered going into business." By then I was in graduate school, moving full-throttle toward becoming a professor.

"I don't know." I shrugged. "I just love teaching."

But I suspect we both knew the real answer. I was scornful of mere money-making, even if it benefited people with insurance against disaster. I aspired to be a Man of Letters like William James, Max Weber, or as I see in retrospect, Heinrich Spiero, the man who owned 16,000 books, the father she spoke of with admiration and awe.

One may forgive youthful arrogance, but filial betrayal clogs the throat.

**

In 1949, there were 40,000 cases of polio, one for every 3,775 Americans, almost twice as many as three years earlier. "Polio Scourge." "Polio's Deadly Path."

Radio, newspapers and the "March of Time" newsreel warned parents to keep their children out of public swimming pools, avoid crowds, and maintain germfree conditions at home. The invisible virus would strike randomly, without warning, from one day to the next turning your frolicking boy (almost always a boy, for some reason) into a boy who would never walk again.

During the postwar decade, Americans feared the red tide of Communism surging across Eastern Europe and China, and feared the dark schemes of Communist spies inside our country, and of course there was the threat of obliteration by A-bombs and H-bombs. But polio was the fear that hit home. Husbands and wives were having children—three, four beautiful children—and the virus wanted to cripple them.

I was nine or ten, eating a sandwich at the kitchen table, when I asked my mother, casually, as if it had just occurred to me, whereas in fact it had been lurking dreadfully in my mind for too long: "Is polio inherited?"

"No, darling," she said, stroking my head, as if she had been expecting the question. "We don't know what causes polio, but it's not genetic."

The dread lifted off my shoulders. I took my roller skates out of the closet, went downstairs, used the key to tighten the clasps over the edge of my shoes, and zoomed down the sidewalk of Forty-third Street, my body vibrating in the one-two one-two beat of metal wheels on concrete, the Lone Ranger and Lindbergh wrapped in one. By Lexington Avenue, though, I was breathing hard, as if pushing against a wind but it wasn't wind, it was something rising in my throat, warm, thick, dangerously like tears. Whatever this was, I didn't want to know. Just let me keep on skating. So I stuffed it back down into oblivion and went about my life without polio.

Now, sixty-some years later, I'm finally ready to drag it out into the light. I lay it on the page, where it squirms away from my pen, skittish, tender. What's going on here? Oh, right: guilt. I was roller skating while Daddy limped with a cane. Well, that's a fair enough judgment upon the boy who liked to believe he was innocent. But wait, that's not the real answer. Because here comes that old emotion lurching up from my chest, hot and scary, and in tears I embrace the sadness, the terrible sadness, that my father and I could never skate together.

***

Life insurance failed him. In cruel defiance of New England Mutual's actuarial tables, my mother died first, age sixty. For two years she battled her way back from one stroke, then another and yet another until in May 1967 she uttered a savage wail from the hospital bed and drowned in pneumonia.

"This isn't how it was supposed to happen," my father said in a voice of stone.

Once again, grim chance had invaded his story. But again he fought back. "I'm planning to marry Adelheit, a friend from childhood," he said on the phone a half-year later. "I hope that's all right with you. You see, I don't want to be an old man sitting in a corner for the rest of my life."

At age twenty, I had sat with Jeanette across from my parents in the living room, asking their endorsement of our decision to get married. Now he was asking me. It was a gesture of respect, grownup to grownup, but I was feeling far from grown. I may have been a husband, a father of one child and a second on the way, a college professor, but I felt as bewildered and self-absorbed as I had in my teens.

"Of course," I said. "I want you to be happy."

Remarriage was the right choice. Adele rejuvenated him, uprooted him to a modern apartment, took him to parties and opera, even induced him to visit the Germany he had vowed never to set foot in again. One afternoon, as he stood in the doorway about to leave for the office, she grasped his ears and kissed him on the lips. I bristled at her imperious style and her dogmatic opinions, but for ten years he was happy and that's what counted.

Personal Histories

He died of lung cancer in 1978, age seventy-two. Afterwards, I wrote this poem.

<u>To my father (1906-1978)</u>

Three days before you heard nothing
I said softly I love you
and you said nothing.
I have not stopped circling
the zero of that silence.
Perhaps the din of concern
arrived before my morning jet.
Perhaps I interrupted
your briefing with death.
Perhaps. I love you. When
did you ever answer me?

After my boy body slid from your lap
and my youth turned out of your hug,
each year our right hands met.
Then you shrank into the bed of cancer.
Your hands wandered apart from your attention
until falling like accidents on the icy sheets.
You fell away steadily smaller
into the appetite of your body, and
I could not catch you. I bent monstrously large
but could not recall how to touch you.
I want to believe we tried. Didn't we?

But you never
read poetry anyhow.

I thought that was the end of it. Of him. I expected my father would disintegrate into a scatter of gestures and sentences, like the snapshots glued precariously in the albums my mother had assembled. To my surprise, he had an afterlife.

Recollecting My Father

When we returned to their apartment after the funeral service, Adele handed me a large, dusty cardboard box. "This belongs to you, now," she said. At home in North Carolina, I sat at the dining room table and pulled out photos, monthly budgets, and best of all, a folder bulging with letters, some carefully folded inside envelopes with two-cents stamps, many in German, most in English, remarkably fresh as they re-emerged into daylight after forty years.

I encountered a father I barely recognized. Here he is, days after he met my mother, courting her with ardor and eloquence. Those 250 words of English have blossomed into a lavish bouquet.

> 3/30/38
>
> Ursula, may be your ears were ringing tonight because I am home all alone, the first time since quite some time, and I am thinking of you (if I may!). I am trying to get a clearer picture of you. Strange this world of ours, isn't it? Just a week ago we met for the first time, and still both of us, I believe, have some conception of each other. Beyond that—instinct might be the right word for it. Be it so!
>
> Much more could be said, and I hope it will. Much more should not [be] talked about, and we will not. I am looking forward to see you next Saturday. And you?
>
> Until then, good night.
>
> Herman

Maybe Hitler and determination and "hunch" had propelled him around other twists of fate, but in finding the love of his life, mysterious "instinct" was in the driver's seat.

Two months after his first letter:

> My dear:
>
> It is amazing that all of a sudden you appeared in my life, that we took a hold each other in such a way without so many words and without any preparation. Or maybe there was some kind of preparation in the kind of life each of us lived before. Or, even there is no need or no place for 'preparation' if we replace it by 'instinct' or whatever you may call it. I told you that I do believe in 'instinct' more than anything else, and probably that's why. . . .
>
> Your friendship and your love, if I have them both, are dear to me. Your confidence, if I have it, I shall try to deserve and keep. And beyond that, we will see as time goes on. Seven weeks did seem long time to us, didn't it, but they still are only seven weeks. Give us time, and we have time! And we will see.
>
> Good night. And my thanks for what you are for me and what you have done for me in being how you are.
>
> Good night!
>
> Herman

I felt a jab of shame reading these letters, as if I were listening at my parents' bedroom door. But that was swept

3/30/38

Monta, may be your ears were ringing tonight because I am home all alone, the first time since quite some time, and I am thinking of you (if I may!). I am trying to get a clearer picture of you. Strange this world of ours! Isn't. Just a week ago we met for the first time, and still both of us, I believe, have some conception of each other. Beyond that — distinct might be the right word for it. Be it so! Much more could be said, and I hope it will. Much more should not talked about, and we will not. — I am looking forward to see you next Saturday. And you?

Until then, good night.

Helen.

Herman Filene's letter, 1938

aside by a sense of pleasure and, yes, triumph. Finally I was hearing my father's true voice, his ardor and longing and hopes.

A few years later, I wove the letters almost verbatim into my novel about a teenager named Murray who, like me, came of age in 1950s Manhattan. But except for being a German refugee, Murray's father turned out to be nothing like mine. Samuel Baum is full of jokes; he leaves his family after a possible affair with his best friend's wife; and he's a Brooklyn Dodgers fan. Well, a novel requires a protagonist more dramatic than a life insurance agent and faithful husband. So I made him up.

On the other hand, there's Murray. Rereading the novel thirty-some years later, I feel as if I've walked up against a mirror. Murray has set out on an obsessive, plaintive quest to learn "the truth" of why his father left, what he's doing in California, whether he had an affair, oh so many tormenting questions asked in pain and love. For his Junior Research Project, Murray decides to write a history of his family. But after reading his parents' letters, and interviewing them and their friends, he only uncovers more bedeviling ambiguities. His father returns home, but Murray can't stop searching for answers. "Maybe you're better off not knowing," his best friend, Ferg, says. "What the hell: he's back. Enjoy him."

As he begins senior year of high school, Murray chooses to follow Ferg's advice. Now I'm ready to do the same with my own Junior Research Project. By a chance that seems too uncannily timed to be chance, while rummaging yesterday in the box of memorabilia, I came upon a letter that gives me what I was yearning for.

February four, 1940.

My dear son:

It may seem strange today, and it will probably seem strange to you many years hence when you will read this letter, that your father addresses you right after you were born. But I believe you should know later what we, your parents, feel today. We all are, after all, only a link in the long chain of our forefathers. . . .

Your mother and I were looking forward hopefully and faithfully to your coming in this world. You are a product of our mutual love. I entrust you today to her care. Love and adore your mother as I do. And be faithful to her. . . .

We shall try to bring you up as an upright man in our country which is our chosen fatherland and which seems today one of the few countries in the world where one can still be 'oneself.' Keep high this flame of personal liberty. Be truthful to our and therefore your past. . . .

All we can do and shall try to do is to give free development to your character and your abilities[,] which are still unknown to us. The day will come when you will judge whether we succeeded. Try then to be fair to us though sometimes you may not be able to understand[,] as we often did not understand our parents. . . .

Your father

Free development to become oneself. What better could any son want?

Be truthful to our and your past. So truth is not only to be acquired, but also to be given.

And part of giving entails being *fair* to my parents, acknowledging that I do not fully understand them.

The day will come when you will judge whether we succeeded.

The letter trembles between my fingers. My father is speaking to me with love louder than the chime of his father's pocket watch. All my life he has been speaking to me, if I listen to the silences.

Herman, Peter and Robert Filene, 1950

Personal Histories

Chapter 3

THE SPIERO SISTERS

(1901-2008)

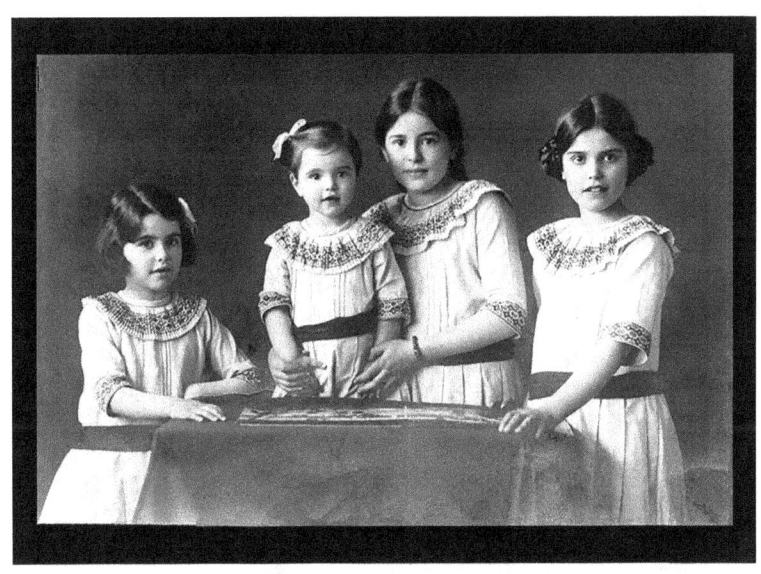

Personal Histories

As the four sisters and their governess strolled along the sidewalk in Hamburg, Germany, passersby made admiring comments. Photographers would stop them to ask if they could take pictures of this beautiful quartet. So my mother recalled with a wistful smile while I, as a child, imagined them as princesses in a kind of fairy tale. Even in this black and white photograph from 1913, they have a glowing presence. My mother sits at the far left, Ursula, seven

Spiero house, Hamburg

years old, known as Usu. Beside her, Christiane, or Kiki, the youngest. Next, Bertha-Sabine, soon calling herself Sabine, the first-born. And finally Josepha, or Josi. The sisters look out at the world with alertness, curiosity, a poise beyond their years, expecting to inherit a wonderful future.

They grew up in a villa in a prosperous suburb, Gross-Borstel, where they were cared for by a governess, a cook, a handmaid and helper, and a gardener. They attended the *Höhere Mädchen Schule von Mademoiselle de Fauquement* (Girls' High School of Miss Fauquement). Their father, Heinrich Spiero, was a manager in his father's shipping company but spent most of his time in his study writing. Poetry, essays, biographies of German authors—thirty books between 1902-1914. He and their mother Olga hosted cultural soirées for illustrious painters, writers and musicians. Saturday evenings, he gathered the family and read poems that his daughters, years later, could still recite by heart. Sunday mornings, he led the family and servants in an hour of religious talk and prayer. Occasionally, dressed in a velvet coat and silk hat, he led the children on full-day "excursions" around the town and lectured about the churches, monuments and history.[1]

It was an enviable childhood, comfortable and contented.

But one year after that serene photograph, the foundation beneath the sisters shuddered. Fifteen years later, it would split open irreparably, scattering them among four countries. To save them from being lost to memory, I'm gathering them together again within these pages.

***

For a century after Napoleon, Europeans lived in relative

peace as their governments formed a complex structure of alliances propped up by diplomacy. Uprisings and brief wars didn't undo the prevailing faith in order and progress—what people called "civilization." But in 1914, triggered by a terrorist's assassination of the Austro-Hungarian heir Archduke Ferdinand, the structure imploded and the Great War began. Civilization became mired in trenches. Progress turned into tanks and mustard gas.

Heinrich Spiero, at the age of thirty-nine, volunteered to serve in the Raw Materials Department of the War Ministry. Soon, promoted to the rank of major, he traveled to conquered territories and confiscated materials for the German cause. In order to be nearer to him, his family moved from Hamburg to an elegant ten-room apartment in Berlin.

At first, their life continued more normally than one might have expected. But by 1917, the third year of war, the British blockade was exerting a stranglehold. German shipping collapsed and with it Heinrich's father's fortune. Nationwide, goods became desperately scarce. Leather was saved for soldiers' boots, so people in line for coal stood in cardboard shoes with wooden soles. Rations of food fell below 1,000 calories a day.

"Turnips," my mother recalled, wrinkling her face with disgust. "Turnip bread for breakfast, turnip soup for lunch, fried turnips for dinner."

When a horse collapsed and died on a street in Berlin, women with knives rushed to the cadaver and fought over the best pieces. Cats vanished from the backyards.[2]

According to Sabine, "we were starving to the point that it was luxury to chew small pieces of leather if we could ever find any. I had eaten all my erasers... We debated seriously whether chewing fingernails was more helpful to overcome the pangs of hunger than chewing blades of grass." Kiki was too weak to stand.³

Their father could have provided his family some of the nourishing materials he brought back for the War Ministry, but that he refused to do. No black market. No violation of loyalty to Kaiser Wilhelm II and the German nation. The war was "a heroic event in your grandfather's life," Sabine explained to me seventy years later.

In 1918, however, heroism proved helpless. As Allied armies and tanks pushed relentlessly closer and German soldiers fell back, sailors in Kiel mutinied. Workers joined them in a revolt that spread to Bremen, Hamburg, Essen, Berlin. A revolution was underway. On November 9, the Kaiser abdicated. That morning, Spiero went to his office in uniform as usual, only to phone an hour later asking Sabine to bring his civilian clothes. On their way home, father and daughter passed men in the street attacking soldiers and officers, cutting off the epaulettes, spitting at them. "Entering the apartment, your grandfather broke down," she recalled to me. "It was the only time I have seen him weeping."⁴

November 9, 1918, Spiero later wrote, was "the blackest day in German history."⁵ The Empire was gone. In its stead, a constitutional convention met in Weimar and established a republic.

***

Before plunging ahead into the 1920s, I need to pause for some uncomfortable doubts. I'm recreating the lives of the Spieros, but what do I truly know about them? Or more candidly, how much don't I know? Hard as I scrutinize those young Spiero sisters in the photograph, they don't come alive. No moods, tones of voice, behavioral quirks—all the signals by which we "know" someone. I'm a century late. Sabine, Josi, Usu and Kiki are gone and have taken their childhood with them. I envy Louisa May Alcott, who enjoyed the freedom to invent dramatic details of the sisterly skirmish among Meg, Amy, Jo and Beth. As a historian, I'm obliged to tread a strict documentary path, following the crumbs of evidence. I have a biography of Heinrich Spiero; a dozen photographs, split-seconds out of the sisters' lifetimes; and my memories accumulated over seventy-some years. Best of all, I have scores of letters they wrote in adulthood.

Yet these letters bring their own problems. The majority are from Sabine, the first-born sister, the self-appointed historian, who assiduously set the past straight and, as I've learned, sometimes told it slant. Which leaves me asking: How do I know which times are which?

For example: She claimed that her maternal grandmother, a Protestant, was baptized Catholic.[6] And this more inflammatory example: In her four-page, single-space memoir of her father in 1986, Sabine declared:

> His marriage had been a deep disappointment to his parents and the family who had expected a brilliant match for him, and my mother was far from that. But he idealized her once and forever and all she did was right and wonderful. This was a hardship for us children and also for him, but he wasn't aware of it.

Kiki, the youngest daughter, the one who faithfully cared for Heinrich and Olga throughout World War II and until their deaths, dissented bitterly.

> How is it possible that my sister … writes such things about our parents' marriage? The day of their first meeting was, again and again, celebrated [by our father] in a modest way. My mother attracted attention everywhere. She was a beautiful woman till her last days and she had a lot of charm and was a splendid hostess.

When I interrogated Sabine, she turned higher the flame of resentment.

> Why was his idealization of his wife a "hardship" for him? Because, whatever she did was right in his eyes, even when she lied, accused him viciously of things she imagined, mistreated her children whom she didn't love because she had desired sons. He never protected us ... nor himself. He must have loved even suffering coming from her.[7]

Here I sit, thirty years later, at my desk in North Carolina, holding these fragile pages, wondering whom or what to believe. How naïve of me to have thought this project would be easy. In my scholarly books —*American Attitudes toward Soviet Russia*, for example, and *Gender Identities in Modern America*—I swept up millions of people into a single sentence. Now, trying to write about four sisters, I'm thrown back to uncertainty.

Still, I'm determined to thread my way among the ambiguities, contradictions and stubborn silences to retrieve my mother and aunts from the past. Once upon a time, I heard their voices, saw their faces. The more I research, the more I want to meet them again and grant them understanding. And like Sabine, I feel a responsibility as the family historian to acquaint my children and grandchildren with their ancestors.

***

The Weimar Republic was built on the rubble of war. One of every five German men were dead or maimed or suffering shell shock. In 1920, the Social Democrats christened a democracy while fending off Communists on the left and embittered nationalists on the right. Beset by the Allies' demand for reparations, the impoverished government steadily increased the currency, which caused an inflation that in 1923 soared into hyperinflation. Prices would jump ten-fold, a hundred-fold, within hours. Some people went shopping with a wheelbarrow of Deutschemarks. Conductor Bruno Walter interrupted rehearsals so that his musicians could buy food before prices rose. Incomes and savings melted into nothing. White-collar workers joined the poor and unskilled standing in line for hours to buy a loaf of bread. "The death of money," people lamented. Only when the government created a new currency, the Rentenmark, did the inflation finally halt.[8]

The Spiero family went unscathed, perhaps because overseas customers of Heinrich's shipping firm paid in foreign currency. Like other conservative members of the intelligentsia, Spiero grudgingly reconciled himself to modern Germany. "One serves the Republic but one does not love it," an esteemed historian muttered. Spiero, who was born Jewish but converted at age eighteen to Lutheran, placed his hopes for the future in "Christian-Socialist" values. Meanwhile, he happily resumed his literary career. Between 1920 and 1933, he published forty books about German authors and culture, edited the ten-volume *Jedermann Lexicon [Everyman's Encyclopedia]*, and was awarded an honorary Ph.D. by the University of Göttingen.[9]

For the younger generation, on the other hand, Weimar culture beckoned with more radical opportunities. Freedom of speech and press. Equality for women, including the right to vote. An outpouring of cultural experimentation: Bertolt Brecht's proletarian drama; the caustic drawings of George Grosz; Bauhaus architecture; political cabarets, homosexual cabarets, and jazz clubs; Dr. Magnus Hirschfeld's Institute of Sexology. The epicenter of this new Germany was Berlin. "The air was always bright, you needed little sleep and never seemed tired," a visitor recalled. "Berlin was so marvelously alive," exclaimed the novelist Vicki Baum, "so enlivened with an unusual electricity." Like in every social upheaval, distraught critics blamed women. "Young ladies proudly boasted that they were perverted," the novelist Stefan Zweig recalled with much exaggeration. "To be suspected of virginity at sixteen would have been considered a disgrace in every school in Berlin."[10] This was the milieu in which the Spiero sisters, each in her own way, came of age.

***

"All my friends and I were intrigued by Communism and rejection of the 'bourgeois' life of our parents," my mother recalled forty years later. At thirteen, she joined a youth group called the *Wandervögel*, the wandering birds. I still remember her tone of voice, vibrant with passion, as she described the longest night of the year, 1919. Along with hundreds of boys and girls she walked through the countryside collecting wood and built a ten-foot-high pile around which they sang folksongs and danced, cooked food from their *Rucksakken*, and held serious conversations. At midnight they lit the fire and saw, on the surrounding hills, some of the other fires being lit simultaneously all over Germany. Usu was one of hundreds of thousands of young Germans who formed a social movement that was more about self-fulfillment than politics. "I grew up and all that in school," one woman recalled, "but I have the feeling that I only came to life in the [*Wandervögel*]." Some participants would later become Nazis, others left-wingers, but either way, they were seeking a sense of community and personal liberation. Liberation especially for the girls. Free of parental control, they developed self-confidence, ambition, and a comradeship with boys.[11] They shocked their elders by wearing short hair and skirts, playing tennis or doing gymnastics, smoking a cigarette in public.

Christiane, Olga and Ursula Spiero, 1927

Ursula was an unruly adolescent. One day when she was fourteen, maybe fifteen, faced with her parents' threat of boarding school, she cut off her long braid and threw it in the toilet. At least so Sabine told me. To doublecheck, I asked Dr. Alice Nauen, a lifelong friend of Ursula's, to describe my mother's life in the 1920s. She gazed at me for a long moment, then shook her head. "I'm sorry, I don't feel I have the right to say."

If only I had interviewed my mother before she died! But in my twenties I was too concerned with making sense of my own life, and then she was gone. Still, there she is in this 1927 photograph, twenty-one years old, short-haired and high-heeled, bedecked with a sequin cape, looking down at her mother while Kiki dances by the phonograph. On the wall, a multitude of unsmiling ancestors gaze upon the playful scene. Were the sisters preparing to go off to a party or a dance, or perhaps the theater? Like all photographs, this one tells nothing about before and after.

We do know, however, about these two young women's behavior the following year, when Bertolt Brecht's notorious *Threepenny Opera* opened. "The *Dreigroschen Oper!*" Ursula recalled. "I think I heard it four times, and we sang the songs at home and shocked our parents. I remember Kiki sitting in the tub, singing on top of her voice one song. . . '*Was ich möchte, ist es viel? Ein mal in dem kurzen Leben einem Mann mich hinzugeben, ist das ein au höhes Ziel?*' 'What I would like, is that much? I would like to give myself to a man just once in this short life—is that too high a goal?' . . . Kiki's loud and lovely voice could be heard all over the place and my father banged at the door and told her to stop, 'what will people think?!'"[12]

Ursula Spiero, 1930

In this photograph, twenty-four-year-old Ursula seems more sedate, but she remained unconventional. Most young German women took jobs as clerical workers until their mid-twenties, when they found a husband and quit. Ursula went to nursing school and became a *Krankenschwester*.[13] Like most professional women, she remained single throughout the Weimar era, enjoying her career along with the pleasures of Berlin.

***

At first glance, her oldest sister Sabine seems to have taken a similarly dissident route. "Mine was the generation," she wrote, "that broke away from [our parents'] traditions as best we could and as far we thought it was needed." But as I've come to understand while working on this project, Sabine became a rebel despite herself. *Broke away as best we could*, but not as she would have ideally wished. *As far as needed*, but not further. Along her path to adulthood, she coped with painful reactions at home and large obstacles in the public realm. Her dissidence was, in both senses of the word, grudging.

To begin with, there loomed her father. Heinrich was formidable, a scholar renowned nationally and abroad while a patriarch at home. Sabine emulated him, which would have been a daunting task under the best of circumstances. Harder yet, she believed she was competing with her mother for his attention. How could she find her way out of this quandary? Her younger sisters, Josi and Kiki, paved an easier route by making conventional life choices. Not Sabine. Exerting intellectual talent and will power as formidable as her father's, she struggled to distinguish herself from him. At the same time, though, she wanted to earn his approval. It would be a precarious course.

She began with religion. At age sixteen, she decided that "'reformed protestants,' practiced a faith I considered whishy-washy [sic] and not a religion." So she became a Catholic. If she hoped to get her father's attention, she was disappointed. "Josi told me that he was happy . . . , but he and I had never spoken about it."[14]

In 1929, age twenty-eight, she decided to become an art historian—not exactly Heinrich's field, but close. Art history was a predominately female profession, like teaching and nursing, but we shouldn't underestimate Sabine's daring.

Until 1908, after all, women had been admitted to German universities only as auditors. When Sabine enrolled in a Ph.D. program at the University of Marburg, women still comprised only one-sixth of all graduate students. Like those in law, medicine, and other professions, almost all of them were single.[15] But Sabine defied that norm, too, by marrying a fellow art student and stage set designer, Hermann Gova.[16] One might interpret this as a way of rivaling Olga for her father's attention.

In 1933, after four years of intensive work, she earned her doctorate, accomplishing what few young women could claim, only to have success slap her in the face. As she recounted to me a half-century later, "When I presented my doctor-thesis to him, published by the Prussian State in a rather impressive folio 'Brochure as a Special Edition of the Prussian State Books of Art,' your grandfather put his hand on my shoulder and said: 'I would have preferred a child.'"[17] A few years later, no one is sure exactly when, the marriage to Hermann ended, leaving her with his surname.

By the age of thirty-one, Sabine had constructed a new and distinctive identity. Born Bertha-Sabine Spiero into a quarter-Jewish household, she now was Dr. Sabine Gova, a Catholic and an art historian. Spurned by her father, she would have to find approval elsewhere.

***

Meanwhile, what were the other two sisters making of themselves: Josi, the second-born, two years younger than Sabine; and Kiki, the last born, five years behind Ursula? For various reasons, I know precious little. Unlike Ursula and Sabine, they lived all their life in Europe, so I rarely met them.

Moreover, Kiki didn't learn much English, so we exchanged only a few letters. Most important, though, they occupy smaller roles in this family history because they led less public lives. Such was the fate of women generally until feminist historians in the 1970s began to fill in the other half of the past. In my books and teaching, I enthusiastically followed their lead. All the more, then, I wish I could recreate Josi and Kiki more fully in the 1920s, but they remain half-hidden within their private lives.

Josi and Fritz Einstein, 1920s

Josi pursued dissidence, but in a direction quite different from Sabine and. Ursula. In her daughter Christina's description, "she was a strappy tom-boy, married at nineteen, knowing nothing of men."[18] Her husband, Fritz Einstein, age twenty-nine, was born to a Lutheran, formerly Jewish family. He had converted to Quakerism. They moved to a rough neighborhood in Hamburg, a far cry from the genteel suburb of her childhood, where Fritz practiced medicine in a working-class settlement house. They had two children during the next three years.

Christina Ilisch, 1930

Kiki may have sung naughty songs from *Threepenny Opera*, but she too settled down quickly. In 1932, age twenty-one, she married a pharmacist, Wolfgang Ilisch, resided in Berlin near her parents, and eventually raised three children. She earned a teaching certificate, but her training at a Pestalozzi school was canceled when Hitler took power.

**

At first they sat closely side by side in matching dresses and demeanor, like fingers of one hand. Now, twenty years later, the four sisters have spread out in seemingly random directions. They are married, single and divorced; professor, nurse and homemaker; in Berlin and Hamburg. That's how lives evolve, one might think. If we believe various psychological studies, however, the plotline is foretold by birth order.

First-born children, like Sabine, typically identify more closely with parents and authority than do younger siblings. They are ambitious, conscientious, and achievement-oriented—miniature adults. Franklin and Eleanor Roosevelt, Churchill and Stalin were first-borns. Twenty-one of the first twenty-three astronauts were first-borns or only sons. (Alas, the research has been almost entirely about males.)

By contrast, younger siblings, the underdogs within the family hierarchy, are inclined to question authority and be carefree. Moreover, having had to deal with older, stronger siblings, they empathize with underdogs like themselves, advocating egalitarian reform. Martin Luther King and Margaret Sanger, for example, were middle children.

The interaction between siblings is equally predictable, according to these psychological studies. To gain their share of the spotlight, younger siblings will differentiate themselves from those above them. This tends to be especially the case between siblings of the same sex. Consider wife and mother

Josi versus professor Sabine; unmarried nurse Ursula versus Josi; and wife and mother Kiki versus Ursula.[19]

True enough. Still, birth order dictates only a part of the story—and not the part that matters most. As we all know if we've lived long enough, events in the world at large propel us or impede us along life's course or sometimes, tragically, upend everything we were counting on. In 1933, each of the Spiero sisters was well on the way toward the future she was hoping for—a quartet of contented outcomes. But that narrative was brutally torn to pieces when the Nazis scattered them across national boundaries and an ocean.

***

The nightmare began within months after Hitler took power. All civil servants and lawyers of "non-Aryan origin" were fired. Jewish students in high school and universities were limited to a 1.5 percent quota. One day in May, 1933, Nazi students in Berlin broke into public and private libraries, threw 25,000 books by "un-German" authors onto the street, and burned them in a massive bonfire on Franz Josef Platz. By 1935, signs appeared on the doors of shops, libraries, theaters, museums, everywhere: "No Jews Admitted." The Nuremberg Laws prohibited marriage and sexual relations between Jews and "citizens of German kindred blood." In 1937, the government pressured Jewish entrepreneurs and shopkeepers to sell their enterprises. A year later, it evicted Jews from their homes.

Who could doubt where all this was headed? Suicide rates among Jews soared. By the hundreds of thousands, Jews desperately fled their homeland for whichever country would take them in: Britain, Palestine, the United States, Argentina,

South Africa, even Shanghai.[20] By 1939, 83 percent of Jews under the age of twenty-four had escaped.[21] But all too many were left behind, thwarted by lack of money and especially by unwelcoming foreign governments. Britain, for example, admitted only fifty Jewish doctors. Switzerland made sure that Jewish refugees stayed only temporarily en route elsewhere.[22]

Heinrich Spiero, born to Jewish parents, was later baptized as a Lutheran. According to Nazi racial arithmetic, however, he was a full Jew, while his wife Olga, born to a Protestant mother and Jewish father, was a so-called *Mischlings zweiten Grades,* or half-Jew.[23] She provided a precarious fraction of safety, enough to keep him from deportation, even as his life turned grim. He was forbidden to publish his writings or hold a teaching job, prohibited from leaving home during the day, restricted to shopping at Jewish stores, and forced to wear a yellow star on his once elegant coat. Still, when offered a job at an American university, he refused to leave his *Vaterland,* benighted though it was.

All of his daughters were three-fourths Jewish, but their circumstances sent them toward different futures.

As the wife of a Protestant, Kiki could remain in Berlin safe from Nazi persecution. When bombs destroyed her parents' house during the war, she and Wolf gave them shelter.

Ursula, by contrast, wanted to escape, but to where? Hopefully to the United States, but with millions of unemployed during the Great Depression, the American government discouraged newcomers. No immigrants were admitted unless they had already secured a job in the U.S. As for German Jews, the Roosevelt administration was unmoved by their plight. But Ursula was lucky. The immigration law exempted a half-dozen occupational groups, including nurses.

Personal Histories

In 1936, armed with affidavits by two refugee doctors in the United States, she secured a visa and arrived in New York as a private nurse. Two years later, she met and married my father.[24]

Sabine followed her, although by a circuitous and treacherous route. Immediately after the Nazis took power, she had emigrated to Paris and found work at the Louvre. When Germany defeated France in 1940, she fled south to the so-called "free zone," which in her case was hardly free. The Vichy regime housed her, along with more than six thousand citizens of enemy countries and Jewish refugees, in an internment camp at Gurs, near the Spanish border. It was a wretched way-station. They were crowded into windowless cabins that didn't keep out rain or cold. No beds, no closets, no plumbing. They slept in straw bags on the floor and used outdoor latrines. Food was scarce; typhus and diphtheria were rampant.

There Sabine waited, week after week, while in America Ursula was working desperately to secure a visa for her. Finally, good news. A Jewish philanthropic organization arranged for three thousand internees to emigrate. Sabine boarded a boat to Morocco, stayed in another internment camp outside Casablanca until she flew to Lisbon, from where she sailed for sixteen days across the Atlantic to New York. In January 1941, she stood on a pier and wept in the arms of Ursula.[25] Now she would have to invent herself all over again.

While Josi's husband Fritz remained in Hamburg, she fled in 1934 with their two children to Holland. There she worked at Eerde, a Quaker school that provided refuge for Jewish and other endangered children. For reasons lost to the past, the Einsteins soon divorced. Fritz and their son Hans emigrated to the United States, while Josi stayed at Eerde with their teenage daughter Heilwig. In 1939, she married a half-Jewish art teacher at the school, Max Warburg, and soon afterwards had a daughter named Lux.[26] "I was conscious, even as a child," Lux recalled, "of the passion between them, of being their love-child, as they often told me."[27]

Max and Christina Warburg, 1941

The Warburgs' refuge in the Eerde school lasted only a few years. On May 10, 1940, "we woke up . . . because the windowpanes were rattling so strangely," Josi recalled, "until we understood that [the Germans] were blowing up bridges, that it meant us, and that now everything, everything was lost."

As the Germans organized the purge that would kill off three-quarters of the Jews in Holland, Max and Josi helped their students escape into the forest. To throw Nazis off the scent, they staged fake suicides by leaving shoes and a farewell note beside a stream. And how were they to save their own children? They got false identification papers for fifteen-year-old Heilwig, and during the next two years they found twenty-two separate hiding places for her. Their only communication with her was via coded messages. To disguise one-year-old Lux's Jewishness, they renamed her Maria Christina. In 1943 they had another child, Iris, who was born with Down's syndrome. When the Germans turned Eerde into a school for "Hitler youth," the Warburgs moved from place to place, living off Max's meager income from cutting trees and digging potatoes.

But liberation was on the way, albeit on the wings of merciless Allied bombardments. One night in the spring of 1944, Josi grabbed Iris from her crib and "I carried her in my arms, and Warburg and I ran under falling timbers, crashing windows and dropping bricks—down the stairs and out of the house. We jumped into a foxhole on the road, and when there was a pause in the bombing, we went from one hole to the other. Under a hail of bullets and crashing bombs I threw myself into the snow, covering the dirty, fearfully crying Iris with my body." A year later, Canadian troops liberated Ommen. At last, Max and Josi could bring Heilwig out of hiding.[28]

Recently I asked my cousin Christina what she remembered of those war years. "Being hungry," she said.

***

During World War II, the Nazis expelled 750,000 Poles eastward, uprooted millions of Slavs, sent millions of Jews to concentration camps, and imported countless slave workers from Central and Eastern Europe. Meanwhile, Stalin deported more than a million residents from Poland and the Baltic republics to Siberia. "Between them," according to the historian Tony Judt, "Stalin and Hitler uprooted, transplanted, expelled, deported and dispersed some 30 million people in the years 1939-43."[29] Even as I recite these facts, I cannot comprehend them.

Four sisters and their families comprise a miniscule fraction of that diaspora, but they bring the stupefying tragedy down to comprehensible dimensions. They embody an imaginable truth. And unlike the wartime dead, their story continues through the next fifty years. More than ever, though, it is a partitioned story. Geographically, the quartet was dispersed among four countries, struggling to keep in touch. As Sabine lamented to me at the age of eighty-nine: "I regret not to know [your children]. There are about a dozen grandchildren of my three sisters, whom I never saw. The evil Hitler did was not ended with his death. Families emigrated all over the world and their descendants don't understand the language of each other anymore."[30] Geographical distance also amplified emotional distance. The built-in sibling dynamic bonded some of the sisters and left others at odds.

Kiki Ilisch, the youngest, remained in Berlin throughout the war, raising three children and sheltering her parents. She was protected from Nazi persecution because of her "Aryan" husband Wolf, but increasingly vulnerable to merciless Allied bombing. By V-E Day, three-fourths of buildings in Berlin were uninhabitable. Then came the Russian soldiers, who were encouraged by their officers to rape German women as they liberated the city. Kiki fled to the countryside and hid, escaping the fate of 90,000 women.

The Allied occupation established order, but couldn't reduce hunger. In the American zone, the official daily ration for adults in 1945 was 860 calories.[31] My eight-year-old cousin Roman went out at night to steal food stored inside American freight trains. Rationing persisted for years. When my mother visited in 1947, she tossed her cigarette butt on the street and a passerby stooped to grab it. When I visited the Ilischs in 1952, I was taken aback by how many potatoes they ate at midday meal. "They're still hungry from the war," my mother explained.

My grandfather was gone by then, but his wife Olga was there, sitting in the corner, a silent and forbidding old lady, at least so she seemed to me. Old she was, but as now I understand, not forbidding so much as traumatized. She had, after all, survived Nazis and bombings and Heinrich's death.

Berlin had been hell, but for Kiki it was home. "I remained faithful to my parents until their deaths," she declared proudly. And beyond. During the rest of her life at 69 Fregestrasse, she raised the children, administered her father's estate, and preserved the Spiero family memories. "She is much more 'family-minded' than me," Josi said.[32] She spent her last years in what her younger daughter called "the old people's home," lost to dementia but generally in a good mood. "It seems to us she feels a little 'at home' by now." Kiki died in 2008 at the age of ninety-seven.[33]

***

The Spiero Sisters

After the war, Max and Josi made their home in England. They found jobs at Dartington Hall, a liberal-minded boarding school in Devon, Josi as head housekeeper, Max as art history teacher. I would meet the Warburg family in England in 1952, age twelve, when I visited with my mother and brother. The experience is as vivid now as it was then.

Josi had a no-nonsense style, suffused with kindness and a wry humor. She was warm and wise. Amid her candid talk and loving spirit. I felt at home.

Josi Warburg, 1950

Max was fascinatingly different. He was slight, gentle, with a wizened face, reminding me of a creature in *Wind in the Willows*. Trained as a classics scholar, he referred to myths and painters I hadn't heard of, yet he did so in a disarmingly casual way. One afternoon, he drew a little shape on a piece of paper and explicated the intricacies of yin and yang. During a train ride through the countryside, he pointed out huge, mysterious clay horses laid down like friezes in the fields by ancient tribesmen. On my departure, he gave me a small leather-bound volume, *The Life and Death of Thomas Woolsey, Cardinal*, published in 1667, as if I might one day be a fellow scholar.

Dartington Hall provided a friendly haven. Even so, Josi and Max didn't find peace. What to do with sweet-tempered Iris, their Down syndrome daughter? With profound reluctance, Max and Josi decided she would fare better in a facility for such children. And then there was the problem of Max. The mental breakdown of his famous, tyrannical father had sparked in sixteen-year-old Max "a flash, the vision . . . kindled by the fire of Heraclitus of Ephesus," which somehow left him incapable of ever finding a focus in life.[34] After his wartime heroics, he lapsed into depression and was eventually diagnosed as bipolar. Neither psychoanalysis nor electroshock treatment stabilized him, and he went in and out of institutions.[35]

Josi wrestled with these tragedies with the same unshakable devotion and honesty that had carried her through the war. She didn't sugarcoat or pretend, nor did she brood or sink into bitterness. As her daughter Christina observed, "she lived so much in the present, and for the future." One hears that tone in a letter Josi wrote me and my wife Erica in 1985.

We were glad to have news about your kids, we hope for more, and photos, when you are here.

May I say how glad I am that you hope to visit Sabine; it is so important, she is the oldest and loneliest (sp?) of us all. . . .

We are all right and hope you'll find us so. I am extremely glad that you are happy—life is short. Also mine seems fairly long already. I was 82! at Easter. Sometimes I feel 28, sometimes 182. Well, that's life.

Take care, dear both, so long.

Josi et al.

(There are plenty GLADS in this letter. Never mind, I AM GLAD.)[36]

During her travails, she turned to her youngest sister. "Josi and Kiki were the real loving, caring, easy, generous sisterly deal," as Christina put it. The two of them had experienced the war firsthand, unlike Sabine and Ursula, and now they lived only Channel-width apart. The Warburgs and Ilischs exchanged constant visits. As Max's mental illness intensified and he and Josi finally separated, she found solace in Kiki and Wolf's stability.[37]

Meanwhile, Josi and Sabine unfortunately drifted apart, not only because of the ocean between them, but especially because the siblings were so different. First-born Sabine studied art history and engaged through ideas; second-born Josi lived in the present and future, and engaged through feelings. Sabine was single and childless; Josi married twice and raised four children. The sisters kept up a steady stream of letters between them, but during sixty years they met face to face only four times. "She sucks the air out of a room," Josi said ruefully.

"She remained a foreigner to me," Sabine lamented after Josi's death.[38]

Sabine Gova, 1957

The Spiero Sisters

***

When Sabine landed in New York in 1941, she rejoined her favorite sister, Ursula.[39] She never forgot her first sight of one-year-old me, "a red screaming bundle," when she walked into our apartment.[40] A half-century later, overcome by nostalgia on what would have been my mother's eighty-fourth birthday, Sabine retrieved from her files a letter I wrote to her at age seven.

> Dear Bi.
>
> We missed you very much. I wish you could stay at our house all the time, kisses and kisses and kisses and kisses and kisses
>
> Peter.

Below my penciled words, Sabine wrote with a shaky hand:

> Kisses and kisses and kisses and kisses and kisses
>
> Bi.[41]

As a child, I found "Bi" fascinating. As I grew older, I felt more resistant. After an hour or two of nonstop theories and medieval paintings, I was gasping for air. Still, we kept in constant touch, two historians, two first-borns, through countless conversations and letters, especially letters.

Sabine surrounded herself with an exotic aura. In vivid contrast to my mother, she wore makeup and colored her hair. She wore high heels, tight skirts and dresses, never pants. She usually arrived late for dinner or parties in our apartment, as if (my father would mutter) the star of the show. And there was her distinctive voice: tuned to a pitch for public speaking; colored by a French accent; constantly, effortlessly delivering information and ideas.

She lived in a one-bedroom apartment on West 58th St., situated—how symbolic!—a block away from the Paris movie theater. Wherever one looked in her living room, there was something striking. The Mexican rugs. The bird cage and little birds fluttering overhead. Photographs of Paris and Venice. Shiny necklaces and bracelets. The wooden coffee-bean grinder whose handle I loved to turn.

Whereas some émigré intellectuals readily obtained a professional niche in America—Thomas Mann, for example, or Albert Einstein and Paul Tillich—the majority, Sabine among them, had to cobble together all sorts of jobs.[42] She lectured about art at the Metropolitan Museum. Talked to civic groups about postwar Europe. Served on the Speakers Research Committee for the United Nations. Wrote for international publications. Hosted a half-hour radio show about art, "More Than Meets the Eye." And in the 1960s "for five short years of my life when I was what I—once and for all—had wanted to be," she taught at two local Catholic universities.[43] Amid this flurry, she traveled abroad—Paris, Florence, Spain, the Soviet Union— and returned with slides and notes for yet more lectures. She also organized a charitable foundation in Haiti, which served more than a hundred destitute villagers and taught clerical skills.[44]

It's an admirable résumé. But some of it she embellished. She told me, for example, she had spent "fourteen years as a volunteer with incurable patients in war and concentration camp."[45] One of her former college students came away believing she had served in the French Resistance.[46] During her visits to Haiti, she said, "Twice I was almost shot down by a *macoute*," a militiaman, only to be saved by presenting a letter from the wife of dictator Duvalier.[47] Such stories may simply have exaggerated the truth. But when she claimed to be the daughter of a French mother, she was making up her past.[48]

"Sabine tells lies about herself," my father said with disdain. The relationship with his sister-in-law was prickly. Her self-important monologues irritated him. He too had been a refugee who had overcome great hardships, yet he rarely talked about his past or himself, and always in modest terms. Much as I value my father's strict sense of integrity, however, I've developed a more tolerant perspective toward Sabine's misrepresentations. All her life she was on her own, a single woman striving for recognition in a foreign culture. As she noted in a letter to me in 1990, "Your career was under a lucky star: one country, one language, one field of teaching. No wars. And you are a man. It's easier nowadays than at my time to be a woman even when you are intellectually gifted. But in 1957, I was the first 'female' at any American Jesuit university."[49] Against these odds, it's understandable that she was tempted to invent herself.

Regardless of my father's coolness, Ursula and "Bine" enjoyed a strong and affectionate sisterly bond. My mother invited her on Thanksgiving, Christmas, birthdays and other family gatherings. And almost every day, at least so it seemed to me, they held long phone conversations. I can still hear the alternating rhythm of my mother's voice and silence, voice and silence, in the living room. "More personal words are spoken on the phone than otherwise," Sabine remarked. "That's the way our family is."[50]

Then in 1965 my mother had a stroke, at the age of fifty-nine. After a year of valiant rehab, a second stroke undid all her work. She spoke in halting phrases. Again and again, she dissolved alarmingly into bursts of loud weeping. My father turned the living room into a hospital room, bought a wheelchair, hired a night nurse and "the girl, Peg, good Irish import," consulted doctors, and fought grimly against fate.

He also struggled with Sabine. She admired his courage and hoped his overcoming of polio would inspire Ursula to overcome the stroke.[51] But she disputed the doctors' advice to ignore the weeping. Better to practice continuous warm compassion, she argued, a method she had learned while in Russia.[52] By the spring of 1967, my father had run out of patience. "Sabine visits mother once a week for one hour and does not understand anything and does not want to," he declared. "I have given up to try to explain it to her." Desperately, he reached out across the ocean and persuaded Josi to help care for her younger sister. "Josi's visit was very nice, she and I got along very well," he reported. "In a way, she now shares the responsibility and knows that everything possible has been done and is done for mother."[53] He could no longer fend off fate. Two months later, Ursula died.

The quartet of sisters had lost their next-to-youngest member, Sabine's favorite, the one with whom she had shared the past quarter-century. The United States suddenly seemed drained of meaning. Alien. At age sixty-seven, she emigrated back to France, but instead of Paris, Castelnau-d'Estrétefonds, a village of three thousand people near the Pyrenees. Why there? Nuns had converted a medieval convent into a retirement center where, Sabine believed, she would find companionship and care in her old age. To her dismay, the other residents were not only in their eighties and nineties; most were sinking into dementia. She felt more alone than ever. As Josi said, "she is the oldest and loneliest of us all."[54]

Once again, Sabine found comfort and identity in words. She gave a lecture in Bourbonne about Spanish art, in Florence about Donatello, and also in Bremen, Berlin and a Benedictine monastery near Kansas City. She traveled through Germany and Holland with a Swiss student and his friends, and "it didn't take three days that my answers to their questions became almost lectures."[55] She wrote a book about the history of Castelnau-d'Estrétefonds. And most of all, she wrote letters. Letters to former students. Letters to two Russian friends who wanted to visit her. One hundred Christmas letters. Letters to Josi and Kiki and me.

In 1985, Erica and I visited eighty-four-year-old Sabine in the convent. After three days I felt the familiar sense of suffocation. She refused to waste time on chitchat, everyday anecdotes, sentimentality, jokes—the stuff of personal conversation. She gave "almost lectures." By this time, however, I finally had developed enough empathy to realize she was confined—trapped—by her hard-won intellectual talent. She spoke English, French, German and some Italian, but she hadn't learned to voice her emotions. Instead of face to face, she delivered her feelings on paper. At ninety-two,

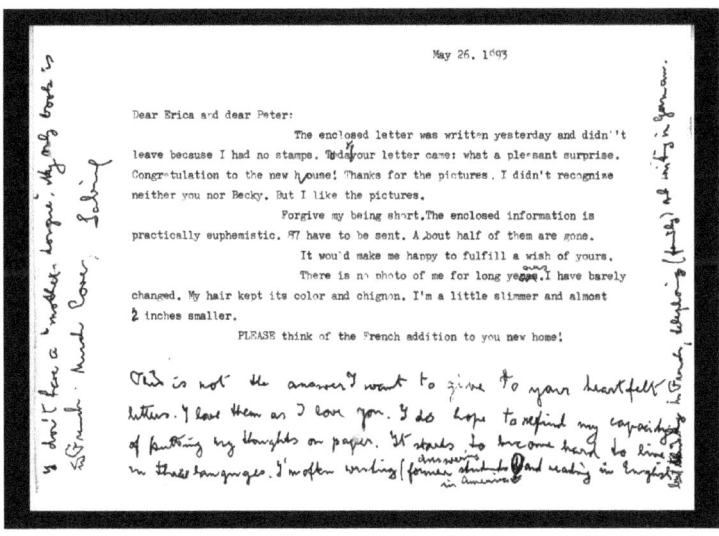

Sabine Gova's letter, 1993

for example, she wrote me and Erica with thanks for "your heartfelt letters. I love them as I love you."[56]

By then, old age was defeating her willpower. "I find this [unsent] letter in the disorder of my desk. I'm sorry but helpless. What it means to be old knows only the person who IS it."[57]

At ninety-six she suffered a stroke that left her paralyzed and, worse, speechless. The nuns kept her alive, until she died at the age of ninety-nine, having outlived two of her three sisters. Shortly afterwards, I received in the mail a heavy box containing her bequest: all my letters to her and copies of her letters to me.

**

While Sabine was constructing a career in America, her younger sister Ursula devoted herself to husband, children, friends and acquaintances, and a myriad of social and intellectual activities. She became—as her stationery letterhead declared—Mrs. Herman L. Filene. Like Kiki and Josi, she led a domestic life, but hers moved at twice their speed. She was an intensely devoted mother, as her fifty-page journal of my childhood testifies. I gloried in her ardent attention. She was also an interesting mother, and as I grew older, I feasted on her interests: Baroque music; the "Family of Man" photography exhibit at MoMA; poetry. I wanted to be interesting, too.

When my parents married in 1938, the Depression was far from over and my father was barely recovered from polio. Money was tight. Still, like most men of that era, he expected her to give up her career and tend the home. After I and my brother Bobby were born in 1940 and 1942, there was more than enough for her to tend, even with the part-time help of young women. Wartime rationing added to the challenges of housekeeping. She found time, though, to walk around to neighborhood shops and collect old keys as well as other scrap metal to be melted down for the military.[58]

Peter, Bob and Ursula Filene, c. 1954

As Bobby and I grew older, Ursula spread her energy wider. She had phone calls, lunches and dinners, parties and outings with dozens of longtime acquaintances in the German-American community. Rudy, Liselotte, Kurt and Brigitte, Ernst, Fritz and Gaby, "some rather boring people in Kew Gardens, friends of Tante Elfriede." Less pleasantly, my father's sister Dorothy consumed a huge amount of attention with her loneliness, resentments, and episodes of severe depression.[59] All the while, Ursula kept her hands busy. She sewed a complete wardrobe for my playmate Laurel's doll, including a winter outfit replete with a coat with white fur collar. She made brownies for the high school fair, and wrote a condolence note to the widow of my science teacher. During the week before Christmas, she closed off the living room and secretly transformed it with colored lights, tinsel, fancy paper over the pictures, a small mountain of gifts, and a candle-lit tree.

While my father commuted steadily back and forth along 42nd Street, eight o'clock to five, Monday through Friday, my mother devised an eclectic agenda. The day of astronaut John Glenn's liftoff into space, for example, she rushed out to buy film and went to Grand Central to photograph the crowd in the concourse watching the overhead screen. "They were silent and tense, there was no laughter," she reported. "If the word 'togetherness' were not such a 'Kitsch' word, it would describe best of all what people felt. I don't think it was patriotism or national pride—it was admiration for this one man's courage—and worry and fear." That evening, she taped a concert on WQXR by Bruno Walter, who had recently died. Earlier that week, she and my father and Dorothy went to "a funny little theatre on 6th street, between Avenue C and D, to meet Hilda and Fritz Levy and Hilda's 81-year-old mother, and they all came here afterward, again for coffee and cake."[60]

There were three constants. Smoking (Pall Malls out of the silver case on the coffee table). Crocheting (scarves, shawls and baby blankets for friends and even, I think, a scarf for the elevator man). And especially letters. She sent letters to her sisters, relatives, friends and who-knows-who-else around the globe. Two-, three-, sometimes four-page single-spaced letters typed at nonstop words per minute. In those pages she recounted whatever was on her mind, whether a close friend's death or the new living room curtains or Fitzgerald's *Tender Is the Night* or (on behalf of someone in Holland) "the names of the Dutch board of the Fulbright scholarship. PLEASE LET ME KNOW, PETE."⁶¹ People often wondered how she found time for all those letters. "It does not take much time to sit down and type a quick letter," she insisted. "Everybody could do what I am doing."⁶²

> MRS. HERMAN L. FILENE   330 EAST 43rd STREET - TUDOR CITY - NEW YORK 17, NEW YORK
>
> February 21, 1962
>
> Dear Children - *Jenny + Peter*,
>
> Every once in a while some friend or relative writes to me, saying, 'how do you find the time for all your correspondence' and I usually reply that it does not take much time to sit down and type a quick letter. (Thinking, deep down in my unfriendly mind that it really does not take much time and that everybody could do what I am doing). BUT: I am not quite as unfriendly and thought less as this may sound. During the past 2 weeks, I experienced an avalanche of work, coming from all sides,and I hardly found time even for a short note to you.Again in() - I try to do all my letter-writing during the day because father does not like it much when I sit and write in the evening. And were my days busy! All this should serve a. as an introduction, b. as an apology for unfriendly thoughts when other people did not write on account of no time.
> I will answer your mail at the end of this letter, individually. Let me start with a description of February 20th.
> We, as probably millions of other people, had not believed anymore that Glenn would take off, had not set an alarmclock and might even have slept longer than usual if the phone had not woken us up at 7.30. I think I fooled the caller successfuly, pretending I had been awake - it's so embarrassing when someone says apologatically,'I hope I did not wake you up, I know you always get up early!' - It was our friend, Mr. Fromm, the butcher, who had been worried about me because I had not ordered anything for 2 weeks. Well, I did not order anything now but explained that we would go away for the long Washington weekend and after many good wishes back and forth this started the day. And then we turned the radio on, heard the beginning count-down, turned the TV on and kept it on - but when father left at 9 o'clock, the count was still 35 and one could not be sure whether this would be the real thing.
>
> Since Sunday, I had opened my'statistical office'in Peter's room on the bridge table - Bellevue Hospital file cards and lists on which I worked for Lehfeldt - and I had to be at the clinic at 11 AM to bring back everything they needed for the clinic that day. I moved the table into the livingroom and with one eye, and both ears on the TV, I started counting and writing. By 9.30, my bloodpressure probably was higher than Glenn's and I discarded work and only listened, quickly called Dorothy to make sure she saw TV(and she did)and when it was ZERO and the mysterious capsule was shot up into space like a ball of fire, I realized I was crying and saying'Oh God' - it looked as if something fiercely alive had been torn away from the earth and was on its way to a'point of no return'. - There have been several occasions when Television was very exciting - be it elections, or UN discussions. But what followed yesterday - conversations between a man in space and people in California, Australia, Bermuda, all this being relayed ** to us in our livingrooms, or stores, or little portable radios on the street, or the tremendous screen in Grand Central Station - to

Ursula Filene's letter, 1962

Growing up, I didn't wonder about her breathtaking busyness. It was what good mothers do, I thought. In turn, I filled my days with work and hobbies, and worried about wasting time, and hungered for approval of my achievements.

Only long after her death, as I began questioning my life-in-constant-motion, did I wonder how much frustration simmered beneath her busyness. If Sabine paid an emotional price for her career as a single woman, so did Ursula, I believe, for her life as wife and mother. "Herman has peculiar views when it comes to money or budget...," she acknowledged. She chafed at receiving a monthly allowance from him and having to record her spending in the *Abrechnung* [budget] down to the last penny. Sometimes she "cheated" to make the numbers come out even. In 1948, wanting to help out Kiki and Wolf in Berlin, she resorted to secretly borrowing $375 from

Ursula Filene, early 1960s

her sister-in-law Dorothy. Her failure to repay intensified the animosity between them.[63]

How much did she regret having given up her career as a nurse? In postwar America, even college-educated women were expected to find fulfillment as homemakers. That was what Betty Friedan lacerated as "the feminine mystique" in 1963. That was what younger women would dismiss in the feminist movement of the 1970s. Fifty-three-year-old Ursula took her proto-feminist steps ahead of them.

In the late 1950s, with both sons away in college, she began volunteer work with Dr. Hans Lehfeldt at Bellevue Hospital. The famous German-born gynecologist, an early proponent of contraception, was conducting a research project about the Pill, using Puerto Rican women as subjects. Ursula eagerly took the opportunity to interview the women and tabulate the data. By 1962, she had converted my former bedroom into a "statistical office," working at a bridge table to analyze the patients' file cards before delivering the results to the clinic at Bellevue.[64]

Meanwhile, she grabbed a second opportunity, this one for pay. A Park Avenue surgeon wanted to hire a parttime receptionist for $24 a week.

"It will be the first time in my life that I go for an interview for a job I don't really 'need,'" she wrote me. "It would be nice earning some money of my own and Daddy very generously offered to pay the taxes," she told me. "If I get the job, and of course keep my Bellevue work and my Spanish studies, I would be fairly busy but not too busy. Also having a real schedule would probably help me getting things done easier than now...."[65]

She was redefining her sense of identity. In 1965, for example, she made a significant choice. My father had found a cheap charter flight and suggested she visit her family in London and go on to Paris for three weeks. She was tempted. "At first I said 'no,' and then I said, 'not without you,' and when we talked more about it, I realized that either way I could not possibly go away now when our [Bellevue] study group is not completed (we have 139 patients, are taking in 161 more, at the rate of about 30 or 40 a month)."[66]

There would be no trip. But tragically there would be no clinic work either. A few weeks later, she had a stroke. The next year, a second stroke. Now she had to busy herself with cruelly rudimentary tasks.

> My life is all circling around the arrival of Miss Greer, who came twice this week and will come again today. And since she told me what to do with arm and leg when she is not here, I am leading a busy life. I have not yet started to read something—in almost four month [sic] I have read two books! But that will change, too. . . .
>
> Peter's room is mine and you would see that by discovering the bars [for walking?] there, 6 feet long, which are taking all the room, leaving just enough space for my typewriter.
>
> Though this seems to be a short letter, it took long to type and the clock tells me that Miss Greer will be here in half an hour. Then I have to be in bed! So—goodbye and HAPPY BIRTHDAY, [Jenny,] and I hope Benjamin will not pick this day for cutting his teeth! Give him a kiss from his grandmother, though he hardly knows her.
>
> A kiss for yourself, from your mother.[67]

My father was a life insurance agent. He knew the actuarial tables. Sixty was wrong, grievously wrong. "I was supposed to die first," he said, bewildered, beaten down.

Who knows what my mother would have made of herself if she had been granted a future beyond dying in 1967. Surely she would have been busy in marvelous and large-hearted ways. I've learned to accept her absence, and yet, again and again through all these years, I've tried to hear her voice in unmade phone calls and unwritten letters.

***

In the months of mornings as I sat at this desk writing this memoir, I accompanied the Spiero sisters to distant times and places: Weimar Berlin, war-torn Holland, England in peacetime, and southern France. They were wrenched apart, and yet they continued—despite wars, disagreements and silences—to keep in touch. Reading their letters, I felt buffeted by their hardships, awed by their courage, and increasingly tethered to them by affection.

Now as I contemplate the conclusion, I'm haunted by a sense of transiency: not only the uprooting from homeland, but the passing through time. Sabine, Josi, Ursula and Kiki are gone. Most of what they did and who they were has gone with them. A handful of people remember them, but inevitably they too will go, taking their memories with them.

This memoir will outlast memories. These words and images are lodged in a computer's hard drive and lasered onto paper so that the Spiero sisters' great-grandchildren may someday enjoy the company of these fascinating women.

Personal Histories

Except where cited, all letters are in my possession.

1. Sabine Gova to Peter Filene, March 1986.
2. Adam Hochschild, *To End All Wars: A Story of Loyalty and Rebellion, 1914-1918* (New York: Houghton Mifflin Harcourt, 2011), 311-12; Matthew Stibbe, *Germany, 1914-1933: Politics, Society and Culture* (London: Longman, 2010), 42.
3. Sabine Gova to Peter Filene, March 1986 and Christmas, 1968.
4. Sabine Gova to Peter Filene, March 1986; on soldiers, see also Eric D. Weitz, *Weimar Germany* (Princeton, 2007), 24.
5. Spiero, *Deutschlands Schicksal und Schuld (Berlin, 1920)*, 63, quoted in Anna Rohr, *Dr. Heinrich Spiero* (Berlin: Metropol, 2015), 48.
6. Sabine Gova to Peter Filene, April 23, 1992.
7. Sabine Gova to Peter Filene March 1986; Christiane Ilisch to Peter, March 15, 1987; Sabine to Peter Filene, May 19, 1986.
8. Claudia Koonz, *Mothers in the Fatherland: Women, the Family, and Nazi Politics* (New York: St. Martin's Press, 1987), 38; Eric D. Weitz, *Weimar Germany: Promise and Tragedy* (Princeton, NJ: Princeton University Press, 2007), 9, 135-42.
9. Hans Delbruck, quoted by Walter Laqueur, *Weimar: A Cultural History*, new ed. (New Brunswick, 2011), 4; Rohr, Spiero, 48-49.
10. Carl Zuckmayer, *Als war's ein Stuck von mir* (Hamburg, 1977), 218); Vicki Baum, *Es war alles ganz anders: Erringerungen* (Berlin, 1967). Quoted in Koonz, *Mothers in the Fatherland*, 43; Zweig, *Die Welt von Gestern* (1942), quoted in Peter Gay, *Weimar Culture: The Outsider as Insider* (New York: Harper Torchback, 1970), 130.
11. Quoted in Thomas A. Kohut, *A German Generation: An Experiential History of the Twentieth Century* (New Haven: Yale University Press, 2012), 50, and 31-32; Ute Frevert, *Women in German History: From Bourgeois Emancipation to Sexual Liberation* (NY: Berg, 1988), 201-03; Gay, Weimar Culture, 77-78.
12. Ursula Filene to Dear Children, May 5, 1965.
13. Frevert, *Women in German History*, 179, 201, fn. 69; Koonz, Mothers in the Fatherland, 437, n. 59.
14. Sabine Gova to Peter Filene, April 23, 1992, and March 1986.
15. Frevert, *Women in German History*, 121-22.
16. Rohr, *Dr. Heinrich Spiero*, 119-20.
17. Sabine Gova to Peter Filene, March 2, 1986.
18. Maria Christina Warburg to Peter Filene, Jan. 19, 2020.

19 Frank J. Sulloway, *Born to Rebel: Birth Order, Family Dynamics, and Creative Lives* (New York: Pantheon, 1996), esp. xiv-xv, 21-22, 68-71, 85-86, 95-96; 298, 266; Brian Sutton-Smith and B.G. Rosenberg, *The Sibling* (New York: Holt, Rinehart and Winston, 1970), esp. chapters 4 and 5; Frances Fuchs Schachter, "Sibling Deidentification and Split-parent Identification: A Family Tetrad," in *Sibling Relationships: Their Nature and Significance across the Lifespan*, ed. Michael E. Lamb and Brian Sutton-Smith (Hillsboro, NJ: Lawrence Erlbaum, 1982), 123-52; and Stephen P. Bank and Michael D. Kahn, *The Sibling Bond* (New York: Basic Books, 1982), 51. Other social scientists, though, dispute the importance of birth order. For example, Dalton Conley, *the Pecking Order: Which Siblings Succeed and Why* (New York: Pantheon, 2004); Avidan Milevsky, *Sibling Relationships in Childhood and Adolescence: Predictors and Outcomes* (New York: Columbia University Press, 2011); Julia Rohrer et al, "Examining the Effects of Birth Order on Personality," *Proceedings of the National Academy of Sciences*, 112, no. 46 (Nov. 17, 2015).

20 Deborah Dwork and Robert Jan Van Pelt, *Flight from the Reich: Refugee Jews, 1933-1946* (New York: W.W. Norton, 2009), 91-95, 140. On suicide rates, 268.

21 Ibid., 127-28.

22 Ibid.,150, 158.

23 Rohr, *Dr. Heinrich Spiero*, 13.

24 Dwork, *Flight from the Reich*, 144.

25 https://en.wikipedia.org/wiki/Gurs_internment_camp; Dwork, *Flight from the Reich*, 232-35; Patricia Lochridge, "The Unconquerable," *Woman's Home Companion*, May 1942.

26 Rohr, *Dr. Heinrich Spiero*, 122-23; Hans A. Schmitt, *Quakers and Nazis: Inner Light in Outer Darkness* (Columbia, MO: University of Missouri Press, 1997), 79-84; Frank Einstein to Peter Filene, Jan. 29, 2020. I'm grateful to Frank for the photo of Josi and Fritz.

27 Maria Christina Warburg to Peter Filene, Jan. 19, 2020.

28 Josi Warburg's 's letter to ?, July 22, 1945, quoted in Ron Chernow, *The Warburgs: the Twentieth-Century Odyssey of a Remarkable Jewish Family* (New York: Random House, 1993), 425, 511. See also Schmitt, *Quakers and Nazis*, 199-202.

29 Tony Judt, *Postwar: A History of Europe Since 1945* (New York: Penguin, 2005), 23.

30 Sabine Gova to Peter Filene, July 14, 1990.

31 Judt, *Postwar*, 16, 20-21.
32 Josi Warburg to Peter Filene, April 28, 1985.
33 Christiane Ilisch to Peter Filene and Erica Rothman, March 15, 1987; Rohr, *Dr. Heinrich Spiero*, 125-26; Karola Buerkner to Peter Filene, Dec. 17, 2000.
34 Chernow, *The Warburgs*, 205-06.
35 Ibid, 511.
36 Josi Warburg to Peter Filene and Erica Rothman, April 28, 1985.
37 Maria Christina Warburg to Peter Filene, Jan. 19, 2020.
38 Sabine Gova to Peter Filene, Nov. 8, 1988 and Oct. 4, 1988; and Josi's remark to Peter Filene. On letters, Maria Christina Warburg to Peter Filene, Jan. 19, 2020.
39 Sabine Gova to Peter Filene, Oct. 22, 1990 "...to recall our childhood when she was my favorite of my three little sisters."
40 Sabine Gova to Peter Filene, Dec. 16, 1982.
41 Sabine Gova to Peter Filene, Oct. 22, 1990. Also Dec. 16, 1982.
42 Anthony Heilbut, *Exiled in Paradise: German Refugee Artists and Intellectuals in America, from the 1930s to the Present* (New York: Viking Press, 1983), 73, 263.
43 Quotations from Sabine Gova to Peter Filene, April 25, 1990. On radio show, Phyllis Battelle, *Waterloo (Iowa) Daily Courier*, Dec. 27, 1957. Other information in *Brooklyn Daily Eagle*, Oct. 2, 1950; *Wilkes-Barre Record*, Nov. 16, 1945; *The News* (Frederick, Md.), May 1, 1946; and an online tribute by a former student, Christopher Bogart, http://becauseihadfalleninlovewithwords.blogspot.com/2010/07/dr-sabine-gova.html
44 Sabine Gova to Peter Filene, Dec. 16, 1978. See also her two articles, "Haiti: The Smiling People and the Old Gods" and "The Ile de la Tortue," *The Reporter*, Oct. 20, 1955, 37-42, and Nov. 17, 1955 39-42.
45 Sabine Gova to Jeanette and Peter Filene, Dec. 18, 1966.
46 http://becauseihadfalleninlovewithwords.blogspot.com/2010/07/dr-sabine-gova.html
47 Sabine Gova to Peter Filene, Jan. 23, 1989.
48 Ibid., and *Rochester Democrat &* Chronicle, June 6, 1943, *Franklin (Indiana) Evening Star,* Dec. 27, 1957, and Waterloo*(Iowa) Daily Courier*, Dec. 27, 1957.
49 Sabine Gova to Peter Filene, April 25, 1990.
50 Sabine Gova to Dorothy Filene, Dec. 29, 1958.
51 Sabine Gova to Jeanette Filene, June 6, 1966.
52 Sabine Gova to Jeanette and Peter Filene, Dec. 18, 1966.

53 Herman Filene to "Dear Four Children," March 3, 1967.
54 Josi Warburg to Peter Filene, April 28, 1985.
55 Sabine Gova to Peter Filene, Sept. 22, 1980; March 6, 1983; Sept. 9, 1984; August 6, 1986.
56 Sabine Gova to Peter Filene and Erica Rothman, May 26, 1993.
57 Sabine Gova to Peter Filene, June 29, 1990.
58 Ursula Filene to "Dear Darling" [Herman Filene], Sept 20, 1942.
59 For example, Ursula Filene to Peter Filene, Oct. 2, 1958, and to Peter and Jenny Filene, Jan. 10 and 17, 1962.
60 Ursula Filene to Dear Children—Jenny and Peter Filene, Feb. 21, 1962.
61 Ibid.
62 Ibid.
63 Ursula Filene to Dorothy Filene, Oct. 9 and 28, 1952; Dorothy Filene to Ursula Filene, unsent [1952]; Dorothy Filene to Adelheid Bleichroeder, Sept. 1, 1949, and Jan. 7, 1951.
64 Ursula Filene to Jenny and Peter Filene, Feb. 21, 1962.
65 Ursula Filene to "Dear Pete," Nov. 4, 1959.
66 Ursula Filene to "Dear Children," May 5, 1965.
67 Ursula Filene to Jenny Filene for her birthday, Sept. 23, 1966.

Personal Histories

Chapter 4

Marriage and Memory

Forgetting a name or a recent experience is a nuisance. Misremembering is a more profound problem. It may cause a jarring collision with one's past or, worse, with one's sense of identity. For fifty years, I had fashioned the story of my first marriage around a pivotal episode that let me alleviate my guilt about having left my wife and children. But as I learned a few months ago, the episode didn't happen. Without it, I needed to re-remember the person I believed I was.

***

One balmy evening in the fall of 1959, Jeanette and I were strolling hand in hand along a narrow street in Greenwich Village, a year into our relationship, six months short of graduating college, talking about our future. We had applied to the same graduate schools. But I had also applied for a

Fulbright grant to study in Paris.

"What if I get it?" I said.

"Then maybe you should go abroad while I get my Master's." Jeanette said. "It's just for a year."

A year! My stomach churned with the dread of venturing so far away, alone, lonely.

"It might be good for us," she said.

I gazed down at her face in the glow of the streetlamp. Suddenly I was overtaken by a whirlwind of emotion. "No, Jenny. I want you." I held her tightly in my arms. "Let's get married," I said against her hair in a voice that thrilled me with its passion. It swept her off her feet and it swept out of sight my anxiety about going to France.

During subsequent years, I often replayed that impetuous moment like the flashback in *Casablanca* of Bogart and Bergman rapturously together in Paris. Look at me, unthinkingly, wholeheartedly alive. Of course the movie is fiction, but as I discovered, so was my Greenwich Village scenario. Memory had betrayed me.

I happened to mention that episode while chatting with Jeanette at a local coffee shop. In the half-century since our divorce, she and I have remained friendly, periodically exchanging news about our children (now adults) and ourselves. When I finished recounting our Village evening, she looked out toward the distance, wrinkling her eyebrows the way I knew so well. "I don't remember any such event. And did you apply for a Fulbright?"

I nearly knocked over my coffee cup. Jeanette is the family historian who recalls our toddler son's love of the first Beatles

Marriage and Memory

album, our daughter's pixie haircut, and our neurotic cat hiding in the basement. How could she have forgotten that pivotal episode in our past?

Driving home, I thought of a way to resolve this clash of memory and forgetting. I dragged the dusty cardboard box out of the closet and opened the Five-Year Diary in which I inscribed my daily thoughts and doings for the eyes of some future historian, who now turned out to be me. Here, I told myself, lies the truth.

"Sept. 2, 1959: Began the many Fulbright application forms."

Yes, exactly as I remembered.

"Sept. 5: We went for a walk in the Village. It was good. We talked, rediscovered each other. I love her, but we are very different. I think she is undecided about us. But she left in tears. I wait. She is confused."

There we are in the Village, yet Jeanette's the one with all the emotions. And what about marriage? With a twitch of uneasiness in my chest, I turn the diary pages.

"Sept. 9: We walked in Village, heard jazz."

A second walk—this one strangely, maddeningly unardent.

"Sept. 29: Finishing up Fulbright application."

Okay, the Fulbright, but where are my thoughts about our future? Where is my impetuous, momentous hug?

"Oct. 10: Studied all day. College picnic in evening. Tentatively proposed to Jen tonight. Nothing definite, but we agreed we won't separate in summer."

Tentatively. The word pierces me. Instead of an ecstatic embrace, a half-hearted offer.

"Oct. 18: A fantastically happy day. Studied with Jen. In evening we talked about us and decided to get married next September."

*Studied, talked, decid*ed: such reasonable verbs. At best, I pluck a little consolation from that "fantastic happiness." As for the Fulbright application, I turn page after page and find nothing. Was I hoping or dreading to be accepted? Did I ever send it off?

* * *

Remembering isn't what it used to be. For centuries, people understood it as a process of retrieval. Memories were stored in our brains like items on a shelf in a warehouse, and when we wanted to recall a name or an event, we searched for it. I'm reminded of those high school afternoons in the New York Public Library when I researched my paper on Woodrow Wilson and the League of Nations. I would fill out a "call slip" with author and book title, give it to a clerk who sent it off in a pneumatic tube, and ten minutes later another clerk would hand me the book. Remembering supposedly went like that. Your mind dispatched a chemical signal racing at incredible speed into a corner of the brain to grab the prize and return victoriously. Or not. Forgetting, so people believed, occurred because our mental retriever couldn't find the item or got lost. Even now, most Americans believe this scenario. When asked if memory is like a video camera, 63 percent of a national sample say yes.

The truth is more interesting and unsettling. Psychologists

tell us that memory involves a process of constructing the past. We piece together the family picnic back in 2011, a softball game, and Buddy's poison ivy into a story. "Remembering is an act of imagination," as one scholar puts it. The more time passes, the more we misremember: the dog running off with the softball, although he had died two years earlier.

What's more, over time we remember the false details as true. In one study, subjects recorded their activities every day in diaries. A few weeks thereafter, the psychologist altered some entries by importing details from a different portion of their diary. Participants accepted between 20 and 40 percent of the manipulated entries as true. Indeed, they *remembered* that the altered version had occurred. As time goes by, misremembering increases. Thirteen years after the original diary-writing, participants accepted as true almost two-thirds of their altered entries. "Context borrowing," that's the technical term. Or call it memory mash-up. We construct pieces of our past into a coherent story, whether true or not.

A Fulbright application, a stroll in the Village, and a burst of romantic passion spark a marriage proposal. And off we go, hand in hand to Harvard, Jeanette to study education, I to study U.S. history.

I was twenty when we married, a month after graduating Swarthmore ("the Quaker matchbox"), ridiculously young, but that's what one did in those days. In 1960, the median marriage age had dropped to a historic low. Love and marriage went together like a horse and carriage. As for divorce, nobody sang about that. Except for a brief spurt right after the world war, the divorce rate remained reassuringly low until 1970.

On a rainy afternoon in a crowded church in Great Neck, we vowed to have and to hold each other until. Next, we installed our furniture, books, clothing, Pippin the cat and ourselves in our $100-a-month, one-bedroom apartment on Dana Street in Cambridge.

***

Why did I misremember how we decided to marry? After writing countless versions of this memoir—or rememoir—I've finally identified the culprit: *romance*. Two intertwined romances, actually. During the ten years with Jeanette, I was various kinds of husband: genial, dutiful, amusing, but also blithely self-absorbed and, finally, unfaithful. After I left her and the children, I felt so ashamed I could barely say the word *divorce* out loud. Well, I would console myself, at least you started out as that ardent lover in Greenwich Village.

To make matters worse, I was embracing another kind of romance, which would also turn out to be false. All through college, even as I majored in history, I wrote poems and harbored the fantasy of being a bohemian artist in Paris like Hemingway, e.e. cummings, and the rest of the legendary lost generation. Whatever my alleged topic in the Fulbright application—and I've long ago forgotten—it was the pretext for moving to the Left Bank. So, Fulbright or no Fulbright, why didn't I go?

A long poem I wrote on the verge of graduate school, "Coming of Age," contained the answer—or rather, what I thought, with youthful bravado, was the answer.

> I first walked in shoes of metaphor
> (a fantastic conceit, perhaps,
> and yet I once dared more)

> past the boys with blue felt caps
> scuffing head-bent to Sunday school.

Two verses later, however, the narrator says

> I have become a man among men,
> must take a position and name it.
> And I hold secret
> my heart's adventure

That was the rueful story line I constructed: poetic impulse vs. prosaic career. I forfeited ecstatic flight because I needed to achieve security. It was like those maps my father obtained from the Automobile Association before a vacation trip with "the best route" marked in red ink. School, more school, job, tenure, manhood. I gave up Paris for Harvard. But secretly, proudly—*in the smithy of my soul,* as young James Joyce's Daedalus proclaimed—I forged the creativity of an artist.

If only I had realized how the romantic secret would undermine me more than inspire me.

***

In graduate school, we apprentice historians were warned: you can't write about the past without evidence. You need newspapers, autobiographies, court records, census data, or best of all— the blue-chip evidence—letters and diaries.

For my research paper in Professor Freidel's seminar, I spent weeks searching for an "original" topic derived from "primary sources." One afternoon in 1961, I rode the MTA across the Charles River to the World Peace Foundation in

Boston. "Do you happen to have any records from before World War One?" I asked the secretary, explaining I was a graduate student. She nodded, as if my tweed jacket and green book bag had already announced my purpose. "If we have anything," she said, "it would be downstairs." In the chilly basement I held my breath as she turned the handle of a large safe, swung open the door, and pulled out a stack of letters, account books, and—she laughed, "can you believe this!"—a bottle of wine. I let out a whoop of triumph. This was my moment of baptism as a historian. Two years later, I would open the December issue of *The New England Quarterly* and gaze in awe at my name in capital letters under "The World Peace Foundation and Progressivism, 1910-1918." My first publication. It was thrilling, even if it wasn't a novel.

I've always felt more secure with the past tense. The dead don't interrupt or walk away. They patiently allow my examination. If they're confused, I make sense of things. In French the historical tense is *le passé defini*, the definite past.

Memory's tense is *le passé imparfait*, the imperfect past. *Je marchais, I have been walking*, left foot in the past, right foot in the present, poised uncomfortably in ambivalence. Remembering does not produce definiteness. As soon as you recall an event, bringing it out of the hippocampus into the prefrontal cortex, it becomes presentized. The event you think you've retrieved is never exactly the one you were seeking. Proust's madeleine moment may well have been a *faux* memory.

Of course, "The World Peace Foundation and Progressivism" couldn't hold a candle to *A la recherche du temps perdu*, but it did stand reliably on sixty-two footnotes.

Marriage and Memory

***

At 8:30 A.M., Jeanette and I lock the apartment door, she drives to Concord Junior High School and I bike to Harvard Yard. At 5:30 P.M., I open the door, block the cat from galloping down to the basement, and greet my wife. As I sit in the kitchen, she cooks dinner and talks about her eighth-graders, I talk about the peace movement before World War I, while a Mozart divertimento plays on the hi-fi. She is intelligent, pretty, cheerful, affectionate. We have each other, we are happy, we never argue, someday we will have children. After dessert I kiss her and go to work at my desk.

Late at night, armed with a glass of wine and a cigarette, I write poems, a couple of stories, even the first chapters of a novel. But eventually these lyrical words become smothered by too many monographs to read, too many seminar papers to write.

"I feel as if there's some part of you I don't know," Jeanette says, and I shrug and change the subject. With sixty years' hindsight, I understand why that young would-be man couldn't reveal his bohemian fantasy. It was like a hand grenade inside his shirt. If he opened up, it would have seemed a threat to explode their marriage. Or just as damaging, it would have seemed a foolish delusion that would shrivel in the light of day. By hiding it, I kept assuring myself that, someday, surely, I would dare to become an artist.

***

It's 1969. I've earned tenure at the University of North

Carolina, Chapel Hill. We've rented a house in Cambridge for the summer, but how different it feels—I feel—from who we were years ago on Dana Street. People are marching along Mass Ave against the war. Hippies are dancing in the Cambridge Commons. It's the Age of Aquarius and I am, literally, an Aquarian. I came here to do research on my second book, but subversive urges stir inside me. The morning after we arrive, I put my wristwatch in a drawer to liberate myself from the tyranny of measuring my progress. "Can you make me a silver bracelet," I ask a jeweler in Harvard Square? He sketches a series of six squares. "Trust me," he says, "it'll look beautiful." A week later I slide the bracelet onto my left wrist and it is marvelously beautiful. When I take walks with my children, Benjamin and Becky vie to hold the bracelet hand. I find myself touching it like a talisman. I will never take it off.

"I feel like a better person, a freer one," I say to Jeanette one night, "with love for more people than ever before. We may be breaking out toward a new life, even outside of the academy."

***

Oh, how smoothly I composed that grandiose, self-serving pronouncement! It may have deceived me, but surely Jeanette sensed I was tiptoeing out the door of our marriage.

She wanted to "make our marriage work" because she was a devoted, responsible person; because we had good times together; because we had two adorable children; because somehow she was willing to forgive my self-absorption; and because she loved me. And yet. And yet, I scorned the dreary plotline of my life. Instead of bourgeois existence in small-town North Carolina, I yearned to write in an unheated garret in Paris.

A year later, the story took a dizzying turn. I fell in love with another woman, or more precisely, we slid step by step into an irresistible excitement. She had a husband and three children, I had a wife and two children, but we were intent on shaking ourselves free. Despite Jeanette's tearful pleas, marital counseling and my spasms of doubt, I would not be deterred from my heart's adventure, not this time. I felt exultant in the fall of 1970 as I moved into the only place available on short notice, which was a shabby "mobile home" in a trailer park filled with noisy kids and dogs and pickup trucks. The oven thermostat was broken and burned things to a crisp. The walls groaned at night in the wind. I saw my children on weekends. Except for one year in college, it was the first time in my life I had lived alone. This was where the shoes of metaphor had taken me.

The affair with the other woman unraveled inexorably over the next year, like a rope being pulled too fiercely at opposite ends. When she moved to a commune in upstate New York, I accused her of betraying me. Truth is, we served each other as convenient accomplices for breaking out of our marriages.

Now I was entirely alone. Sometimes I felt exuberantly free, starting over, everything fresh and possible. Perhaps I would meet Stephen Daedalus' "strange and beautiful seabird" girl, who would fling open the doors of my life. Perhaps I would rent a Paris apartment and write an extraordinary novel.

Sometimes I felt frightened, because how could I explain to my children why I left them, and god help me, what if Jeanette moved away and I lost them? And seeing her stricken face on Sunday afternoons when I returned them to her apartment, I felt like a brute, as if I had punched her, this woman I believed I had once wooed in Greenwich Village. And four days a week, I walked into my classroom and taught my students about American history.

It was a quandary of my own making. Romance hadn't overtaken me. I had taken it as a delusion about entering my marriage and an excuse for leaving it. Until I faced up to my part in constructing the story, until I became a more honest historian of my *passé imparfait*, I wouldn't escape the quandary. But that would take time. Years of time.

Sources:
Edmund Blair Bolles, *Remembering and Forgetting: An Inquiry into the Nature of Memory* (New York: Walker and Company, 1988).
Christopher Burt, Simon Kemp and Martin Conway, "Memory for True and False Autobiographical Descriptions,"*Memory*, vol. 12, (5) (2004), 545-52.
D. J. Simons and Christopher F. Chabris, "What People Believe about How Memory Works: A Representative Survey of the US. Population," *PLoS One*, vol. 6 (8) (2011).
James Michael Lampinen and Denise R. Beike, *Memory 101* (New York: Springer Publishing, 2015), chapters 3 and 6.
Timothy N. Odegard and James M. Lampinen, "Memory Conjunction Errors for Autobiographical Events: More Than Just Familiarity," *Memory* 12 (3), (2004), 288-300.

Chapter 5

HARVARD DAYS

I was admitted to Harvard in 1960 but I was not a "Harvard man." That title was colloquially reserved for undergraduates. We graduate students occupied some indeterminate, unglorified status, even lower than the "Cliffies," in residence but not true citizens. But at least we enjoyed the blissful privilege of entering the stacks of Widener Library.

I climbed the two flights of stairs past the John Singer Sargent murals, walked between the rows of card catalogue drawers, and arrived at the desk of the gatekeeper. She scrutinized my stack card and waved me on through the narrow doorway. I paused to inhale the musky smell of old books and leather bindings, centuries of scholarly aroma. Ahead, a corridor of rows of floor-to-ceiling shelves stretched as far as I could see. And this was only one of ten floors. The call numbers on the spines of books were strange: neither Dewey Decimal nor Library of Congress, a code I didn't recognize, befitting a university older than not only Melvil Dewey, but the American republic. Whereas the LC system is abstract, grouping books according to their discipline, Widener's is empirical, focusing on their language, place and time. "Aus" contained shelves about the Austro-Hungarian Empire, "C" the Church History and Theology, "Ott" the Ottoman Empire.[1]

The end of the corridor was not the end. I turned and looked down a corridor even longer than the one I had traveled. And at the end of that corridor I turned again to see a third corridor. A ten-floor-high horseshoe of some three million books. More books than I could read in a hundred lifetimes. I felt exultant and frighteningly small. Eugene Gant, Thomas Wolfe's protagonist in *Of Time and the River*, "prowled the stacks of the library at night, pulling books out of a thousand shelves and reading in them like a madman. The thought of these vast stacks of books would drive him mad: the more he read, the less he seemed to know—the greater the number of the books he read, the greater the immense uncountable number of those which he could never read would seem to be."[2]

A week later I was assigned a desk and a little bookshelf (the junior version of the office I hoped to have in my first job) on the seventh floor of the stacks where, during the next five years, I would write three seminar papers, one of them published in *The New England Quarterly*, and a doctoral dissertation, and all the while, I secretly felt like an imposter.

Worse, I had hidden the secret so carefully that I didn't know it was there at work inside me.

***

Harvard Days

In my senior year of high school at Manhattan Friends Seminary, I applied to several small liberal arts colleges and, grudgingly, at my father's urging, to Harvard. "Harvard's the best, right?" he said in one of his typical declarative questions.

I wish I had been grateful for his confidence in me, proud of his pride. But it felt like a heavy arm upon my shoulders. During my campus tour of Harvard, I watched students scurrying through the snow to class, hunched against the biting wind. "Sure, it's really competitive here," the guide remarked, "but you get used to it." At what price the best, I asked myself? One sunny weekend I visited Swarthmore College, 750 students, Quaker like my high school, a larger home away from home.

Rather than argue with my father, I chose passive resistance and hoped that fate would deliver Harvard's rejection. On April 1, the first college letter arrived: acceptance by Swarthmore. Amid my parents' congratulations, however, I stiffened as I thought: what about Harvard? Fate was proving tricky. That evening, I sat down with them in the living room and announced, "I want to withdraw my Harvard application."

"What's the harm in waiting?" my father said.

"But I want to go to Swarthmore."

"It would be good at least to hear you'd been accepted."

I shook my head.

"And who knows," my mother said, "you might change your mind."

These were reasonable objections. But I was contending with the unreasonable, a bewildering churn in my chest. Emotions were for me a foreign language. I could translate

Virgil more easily than my motives and fears. Murkily, though, I understood that a thick envelope from Harvard would ensnare me in a quandary. Only an idiot would turn down Harvard, after all, and I was supposedly smarter than smart, a "genius" according to that IQ test my mother had me take at age seven, the son she called "special." On the other hand, a thin envelope politely saying "We regret to inform you...." would confirm that I would never live up to the person I was supposed to be. Without quite understanding what I was doing in that living room, I performed a little jujitsu and dodged the fateful option. I withdrew the application.

So why, four years later, was I here, standing awestruck in Harvard Yard on the red bricks along which John Adams and William James and Franklin Roosevelt had walked to class? Because it was the next stop on what I presumed was the uphill itinerary of my life. And now I was ready to brave it.

It would be chillier than I had expected—and I don't mean those long Cambridge winters. Harvard professors hovered out of reach, on a podium lecturing to two hundred students or behind closed office doors writing their next book or on leave. In Emerson Hall, Oscar Handlin—squat, impassive, like an owl with black-rimmed glasses— welcomed us to American Social History since 1865. "You'll notice that seven of the eight books assigned in the syllabus were written by Oscar Handlin," he said in a nasal monotone. "I happen to agree with what he has to say." In Harvard Hall, I scribbled into my spiral notebook the eloquent sentences of young Bernard Bailyn as he unfurled, like a magnificent tapestry, the origins of the American Revolution. Arthur Schlesinger was in Washington, D.C., advising President Kennedy. Of all the professors, I thought I would become most acquainted with Stuart Hughes because I was one of twelve students in his French history seminar. Week after week I handed him another few pages of my research paper on "Leon Blum: Reformer or Revolutionary?" Strangely, though, even when I sat across from him in his office, Hughes seemed a bit removed, abstracted behind the lenses of his glasses.

Some of my fellow students also hovered just beyond my reach. After an interesting conversation with David Caute, a graduate of Oxford University, I invited him to dinner with me and Jeanette at our apartment. But the more David talked about his recent novel and about his play to be produced next summer at the Edinburgh Festival, the more provincial I felt with our genial anecdotes and Jeanette's casserole in our little kitchen. I was more comfortable with Patrice Higonnet and his beguiling French accent. As a newly minted Harvard graduate, he offered insider advice on courses and Cambridge during coffee at Hayes Bickford. But one afternoon, when he remarked that, of course, he expected to be hired as a tenure-track instructor at Harvard, I felt the sting of being a foreigner. Indeed, today on the Harvard website I find Patrice's face, elegantly wrinkled under a crown of silver hair, "the Robert Walton Goelet Research Professor of French History, Emeritus."

The example that sticks in the throat of memory took place at a dinner party of three graduate students to which Jeanette and I had been invited. Actually, *I* had invited *us* after I encountered Suzanne in the library, admired her curvaceous body in a skin-tight outfit, and mobilized my charm to extend the conversation into a social get-together at her and her husband's apartment. Picture a dining room table adorned by candles and a platter of roast beef. Many glasses of wine are emptied. Witty sentences ping pong among Suzanne and her husband Peter and their friend Marshall. I am thrilled to be part of this. Midway through the crème brulée, Marshall undertakes an elaborate story that he brings to a triumphant climax with a punch line in French. They burst out laughing. Jeanette and I exchange a startled glance. Did I join the laughter, pretending I understood? I hope not, but likely I did. Certainly I remember the heat of humiliation throbbing on my face as Jeanette and I walked home.

So much for sexiness and sophistication. Within the world of Harvard there was a sphere where, no matter how hard I worked or how deftly I charmed, and even if I somehow shed my layers of self-doubt, I would never be allowed to enter.

"When I like men I want to be like them," F. Scott Fitzgerald confessed. "I want to lose the outer qualities that give me my individuality and be like them."[3]

If I didn't want to be those men, whom should I look to? Fortunately, most of my classmates and their spouses were accessible, congenial people; many became close friends. I shared a study group with some of them. Jeanette and I picknicked with them by the Charles on Sunday afternoons. We joined them at lectures by visiting celebrities like Norman Mailer and James Baldwin. Perhaps these classmates felt like imposters, but I never thought to ask.

When it came time to choose a dissertation adviser, I steered clear of the big-name professors in favor of Frank Freidel, who had recently arrived at Harvard by way of Wisconsin, Shurtlef, Maryland, Penn State, Vassar, Illinois, and Stanford. He wasn't my kind of historian. He specialized in American politics rather than ideas or society, assembling facts into sturdy narratives, not given to theories or metaphors. During the next two years, we had brisk ten-minute conversations in his office. Basically, I was on my own as I wrote about

American attitudes toward Soviet Russia, 1917-1933. It wasn't the classical model of mentorship, which turned out to be just as well. "The funny thing is," Freidel said after reading the three-hundred-page manuscript, "I didn't think this was a doable topic, but I was wrong."

In other ways, ways that mattered to me, he was the perfect adviser. He was unpretentious, affable, with a rumpled suit and a shock of straw-colored hair and a wide grin, willing to chat about his family and ask about mine. He was, in short, a *Mensch*. I felt safe with him. Only years later would I recognize the deeper motives that had led me to Freidel. Reading *The New York Times* obituary in 1993, I learned that he was a Quaker. And surely it wasn't mere coincidence that he was working on the fourth volume of his biography of Franklin Roosevelt, my father's hero.

***

"I think we are all of us a pretty milky lot,—don't you?" John Dos Passos, freshly minted Harvard graduate, wrote a friend during World War I, "with our tea table convictions and our radicalism that keeps so consistently within the bounds of decorum—Damn it, why couldn't one of us have refused to register [with the draft board] and gone to jail and made a general ass of himself? I should have had more hope for Harvard." Dos Passos enlisted in the Ambulance Corps and, while working in a village in France, felt "the drunken excitement" of an artillery bombardment.[4]

Forty-five years later, a war was taking place in Alabama, North Carolina and other southern states. White mobs attacked black and white Freedom Riders on segregated buses. White sheriffs beat and threw into jail black people trying to register to vote. These young people were making history, not studying it. So when some friends invited me in 1962 to attend a meeting of the Congress of Racial Equality, I ignored all the schoolwork awaiting me and said "yes," as if I'd been waiting for this opportunity to venture outside Harvard's breathless sphere.

On Tuesday evening I sat in the backseat of Dick and Gretchen's VW as we crossed the Charles River, passed the Boston Common, and drove down Blue Hill Avenue into Roxbury. The streets and faces turned darker. In the church meeting room, a dozen people sat on folding chairs in a circle, like a Swarthmore seminar, except four of them were Negroes. After a round of names and hellos, they proceeded to describe recent incidents of discrimination and debate strategies for legal as well as direct resistance and I felt like a freshman who had dropped into the middle of an upper-level course. State law prohibited assignment by race in public housing, but Boston projects were almost all-black or all-white. "Let's file a lawsuit with the Commission Against Discrimination," said Alan Gartner, the white school teacher who chaired the group. "Waste of time," a black man said. "Better to hit the First National Bank, where the only Negroes you see are sweeping the marble floor." "Investigate before you demonstrate," a white woman said. Her friend was a teller there and could tally black and white employees.

"Are you coming back next week?" Alan asked me as we were folding the chairs.

Yes, CORE's classroom would take me out into the world where I hoped to make something happen. But first I would have so much to learn not only about the ugly role of race in Boston, but also, to my dismay, about the uneasy place I occupied.

Harvard Days

Northern racism was as pervasive and punitive as down south, but it operated more discreetly. I smelled it in the hallways of the Mission Hill public housing project—urine and fried food—and heard it through the tumult of TV and kids whose weary black mothers said the rent went up ten dollars but that broken window never got fixed all winter. I exposed racism as a tester for Mrs. Fleming. When she answered an ad for an apartment in a white neighborhood, the realtor said, "Sorry, it's already been taken, but we have a good one on Ruthven Street" in a black neighborhood. When I arrived an hour later with the same credentials, the apartment was available. Armed with the proof of discrimination, we confronted the realtor, who said people want to live with their own kind and he had a business to run. We reported him to the Commission against Discrimination, but as usual, nothing changed.

Sometimes the racism burst into the open. "My daughter was beaten up by two Negro kids," a white woman yelled as we picketed outside a store. "Send the Jews to Israel and the Negroes to Africa and let us whites be." The battle for equality was arduous, confrontational, at the edge of risk, and I was excited to be on the front line.

But one afternoon I realized my place was ambiguous. Frank, a black CORE member, and I sat down with the white manager at Sears to discuss their hiring practices. "I get why Frank's here," the manager said, and then he swiveled toward me. "But what are you? Yankee, Irish, Italian, or Jew?" I felt flustered, my face flaring hot. This was a trick question. I was none of the above. My father was a nonbelieving Jew, my mother a Lutheran, and I a nothing with Quaker inclinations. But that wasn't one of the choices. The best I could do was shake my head. Later, in the car driving home, I thought about answers I could have given him. A newcomer from New York. A commuter from Harvard. An outside agitator. All true, but all provisional, like an immigrant who hadn't passed his citizenship exam.

Some months later, at the end of a CORE meeting, I had an even more disconcerting conversation. "You're a graduate student of history, aren't you?" a black woman said. "Well, then, would you come to my Sunday School class and teach the kids about black history." I stared at her for a long moment. Slavery, of course there was slavery, but what else? As my mind raced from the American Revolution to the Progressive era to the Cold War, everything I knew was blindingly white. "I'm sorry," I mumbled. "I'm busy on Sunday." I hurried out the door, trying to hide my shame. Bad enough to be struggling to prove myself at Harvard. Here at CORE I turned out to be a historian who didn't know more than the basics of the history of black Americans.

Where did I belong? Twenty of us were picketing in Dorchester, marching and singing in unison, "Ain't Gonna Let Nobody Turn Me Round" and "Keep Your Eyes on the Prize." Someone leaned out of an upstairs window and poured a bucket of cold water on our heads and we sang louder. Joyfully. "We shall overcome, some day. Deep in my heart, I do believe." The singing filled me with an elation that was the closest I've ever come to religion. I belonged to The Movement. We were crusading nonviolently to bring whites and blacks together, hand in hand, some day, some day.

During 1962-63, I not only attended Tuesday evening meetings. I began doing CORE work on Saturdays, sometimes Sundays, occasional weekdays. Strategy meetings with the ACLU, the American Friends Service Committee, and the Boston Fair Housing Federation; door-to-door leafleting in black neighborhoods; hours upon hours of picketing. At the same time, on the other side of the river, I was busily studying American attitudes toward Russia from 1917 to 1933. You might wonder whether I felt conflicted about devoting myself to a place and time so remote from Roxbury—a "summer soldier in these times that try men's souls," to quote Thomas Paine. Yes, there were occasional twinges, but I had enlisted in the Ph.D. program, and the fact is, I enjoyed the work. I read every article about Russia in the *New York Times*, 1917-1920, took notes on at least fifty books by visitors to "the Red Experiment," searched through 110 boxes of a Kansas editor's papers at the Library of Congress, and wrote two chapters. Not to mention teaching two undergraduate classes and, every week or so, grading sixty-five papers.

Amidst all this coming and going, reading and writing and doing, I also tried to pay attention to being a husband. Jeanette and I walked around Fresh Pond with our best friends, Elie and Bill. Late at night we had long talks about teaching, civil rights, our hopes and goals. We made love. When the Graduate School of Education offered her a yearlong grant that paid less than her teaching salary, I said "don't worry; take it." While I was in Chicago and Washington doing research in the archives, I missed her terribly. We looked forward to having a baby. "I hear every now and then of another divorce among friends our age," I told my journal in the fall of 1963. "I used to be astounded; now I am distressed, but resigned. Our own marriage (and that of *most* of our friends) is stronger than ever." I had occasional fantasies about being free, writing a novel in Paris, but I kept those to myself.

Reading my journal now, in leisurely retirement, I ask: how in hell could any one person have accomplished all this? Maybe two people, one on each side of the Charles River.

But of course, impostors have to run extra-fast to outrun the whispers of self-doubt.

* * *

Civil rights protest was surging nationwide, and our CORE chapter surfed the crest of the wave. Forty people came to meetings, sixty, a hundred, more and more of them black people from the neighborhood. By now I was an old-timer, but I remained an outsider. When I mentioned postponing a topic "until next semester," a few blacks snickered at this schoolboy. One evening, a young black guy insisted CORE needed to set up two employment committees, one in Roxbury, one outside the ghetto, because "you Cambridge people don't understand us. My mother was hit in the face with a bottle by a white policeman." Alan, the chairman, wanted to focus our energy on Boston's notoriously segregated schools. New, young black members demanded action against the price of goods in Shapiro's drugstore and police brutality. They formed a group called Now Now.

In September 1963, we voted to stage a sit-in—our first sit-in—at Wattendorf Realty in Dorchester—with three sit-inners: Betty, a white housewife; Bob, a black student at BU; and as spokesperson, me. *This is it*, I thought. *I'm doing something real.* I dressed in my wedding suit and stashed in the pockets a roll of lifesavers, a brownie and my pipe (I smoked a pipe in those days). At four o'clock on a cool Tuesday afternoon, we quietly took our places on the uncomfortable chairs in Mr. Wattendorf's shabby front office. For six hours, we ignored his muttered threats and listened to the picketers singing outside, and tried to ignore our bladders. "We realize we're breaking the law," I told a reporter, "but we'll do so until

Harvard Days

Negroes are accommodated." At ten o'clock, Wattendorf called the police. Now things happened quickly.

"Okay," a policeman says, grabbing my arm, "let's go." He pushes me out the door and I flinch in the cold air and the glare of flash bulbs. A jolting ride to the police station, a terse clerk, papers to sign. I empty my pockets, hand over my tie, belt, glasses and pipe, and follow a policeman downstairs. "So you got a cause, do you?" he says in a genial tone, as he holds open the cell door.

"Yes," I say, gladdened by his interest. "Did any of it come through to you?"

He shakes his head. "No," he says, "it don't penetrate to me at all, Peter," and slams the iron door behind me.

As I lie down on the wooden bench with my jacket rolled into a lumpy pillow, I feel stunned. I am unfree. Cut off from Jeanette, my friends, the outside world. At the mercy of jailers and, soon, a judge. The stony silence is broken occasionally by banging and faint cries. Compared to SNICK workers beaten bloody and packed into stifling jail cells in Mississippi, this is tame. Still, jail is jail.

After a breakfast of egg on bread, a doughnut, and watery coffee, I sit in court among three men arrested for drunkenness and two for assault and battery. "Plead *nolo contendere*," the CORE lawyer advises me. "It means you don't accept or deny responsibility for what you did, and you agree to accept punishment."

"But I *do* take responsibility. I want to explain why we sat in and then take the consequences."

"Believe me, Peter, you don't want to have a criminal record all your life. Plead *nolo* and keep quiet."

When my turn comes, the judge lectures me for behaving irresponsibly, tells me to live up to my privileged opportunities, and fines me twenty dollars for trespassing. I bite my tongue. Outside the courthouse, Jeanette and friends greet me with hugs and congratulations. "Look at you," they say, and there

Peter Filene, newspaper photo, 1963

Harvard Days

I am on the front page of the *Boston Record-American* in the grip of the husky cop. It's the first time, the newspaper article says, racial demonstrators have been arrested in Boston.

At home, as I shower and shave and put on my regular clothes, I keep being dislocated by that photograph, the public version of myself. In contrast with how courageous I felt in the jail cell, this person appears bewildered, rumpled and very young. He looks like a trespasser. When I walk on campus, the sense of doubleness grows worse. A presence pursues me step by step, jostling my shoulder. I have acquired a reputation. *Nolo contendere* erased the mark of guilt, but I've broken the law. I have the crazy thought that my professors, and maybe my classmates, will disown me for dishonoring Harvard.

Such grandiosity! The history department secretary talked about the weather. In the coffee room, grad students complained about problems in their research. The woman at the entrance to the Widener stacks glanced at my card and waved me on. It was as if nothing had happened last night in Dorchester.

I enjoyed one surprise, though, when Professor Freidel shook my hand. "I'm glad you did what you did, Peter."

And the busy river of day to day rushed on.

***

"There's no poetry in working for CORE," I lamented to my diary as 1964 began. "I have been a historian, a civil rights worker, a husband—but not a writer or dreamer. CORE is remorselessly factual, pedestrian, uninspired." I felt guilty confessing that. But I was learning that guilt would sustain me only so far, like a shot of adrenaline. The true activists—Bob Moses, Ella Baker, and so many others—were single-mindedly, irreversibly dedicated to the Movement, regardless of mobs, setbacks, and the drip, drip, drip of everyday tasks.

Toward the end of the year, after completing my dissertation, I translated my discontent into a poem.

> Thrusting a furled umbrella,
> The young Harvard scholar
> Poles up the sun-crested steps
> Of young dead Widener's library,
> Slips between the granite teeth,
> And is swallowed.
> Wait. A year or decades
> Later he will be disgorged,
> Perhaps plump with facts
> Or pressed between the lids
> Of a monograph—in either case,
> A mute figure cast upon a foreign shore.

By then I knew where I found fulfillment. Not in Widener, not in Roxbury, but in the classroom. My classroom, where I taught my students.

On a cool fall afternoon in 1962, I had stood in the Yard among the hundred or so other new Teaching Fellows listening to the Dean of Arts and Sciences. "Now I'm sure you're nervous about this undertaking," Franklin Ford said, "but don't worry. Just imitate your best teachers and you'll do fine."

I was plenty nervous but I knew that imitating Professor

Hughes or Handlin or Bailyn would be a ludicrous charade. Whoever I might be as a teacher, I didn't want to be them. Fortunately, I had a better mentor than Dean Ford. I was one of the dozen new teachers assigned to Professor Harold Martin, who supervised General Education A, the freshman course in composition and critical thinking. Martin didn't recommend imitation. He provided pedagogy. Every Monday afternoon, he assembled us in the basement of Loeb House to hear our questions and discuss his multipage mimeographed handouts for the coming week. It was a teaching workshop. An underground conspiracy.

This is what I had been waiting for, ever since that evening when I was sixteen, moody, too restless to finish my homework. "I'll be back soon," I told my parents, and I walked to the end of Forty-third Street and gazed out across the East River. *What do I want to do with my life*, I asked? Cars raced along First Avenue. The cold wind curled inside my jacket. Suddenly, the answer came to me, like a telegram delivered out of the darkness. Teaching! I wanted to teach. I didn't know whom I wanted to teach—high schoolers? college students?—or what I wanted to teach them. But I must become a teacher.

The first day I stood in front of the class of twenty Harvard freshmen, I braced my shaking knees against the lectern. I was barely older than they were, which my tweed jacket didn't fully disguise. "Hey," a student had said as I walked into the classroom, "what do you know about the instructor?" The first few months I made every mistake in the book. My lesson plan for Thoreau's "On Civil Disobedience" consisted of twenty-four questions that I asked in sequence, two minutes each. I returned students' one-page essays with scribbled fussy corrections and a page-long commentary in red ink. But it was my classroom and I was ecstatic. In his soft voice, puffing on his pipe, Dr. Martin trained me in the basics of how to become the teacher I aspired to be. That would take years. Decades. But there was hope. At the end of the first semester, a student handed me a penciled note. "Mr. Filene. We all admired the enthusiasm with which you taught Gen Ed. It could have been a dull, non-benefitting course, but it wasn't. Thank you."

Shortly after I finished my dissertation, I was given an even more influential pedagogy, this time not in a basement but in a building outside of Harvard Yard. Symbolic geography. Professor Don Oliver, Jeanette's former mentor in the Graduate School of Education, offered me a job. He was in his mid-thirties, balding, rumpled, more inclined to holding a debate than a conversation, and as I soon realized, he was a man with large ideas. His collaborator, Fred Newmann, was almost as young as me, neatly attired, and quietly astute. They were completing an ambitious social studies curriculum for high school students. They presumed that I, a history Ph.D., brought the tools and knowledge to write case studies about the American Revolution, slavery, industrialization and other episodes. What luck! To be working with innovative educators, to be writing history, and to be paid for it!

But my good fortune went far beyond—no, far deeper than—those pleasures. During the next eight months I acquired a philosophy of teaching that I would take into my classrooms over the next forty years. If Dr. Martin had taught me the *how*, Don and Fred prodded me to figure out the *why*. Why teach about Andrew Jackson, they asked me one day at lunch? Because he was an important President, I said; you can't leave out Andrew Jackson. Why was he important, they persisted? Because of Jacksonian democracy, I said, and his war against the Bank of the United States. More important than the telegraph, Don asked? Or the cholera epidemic, Fred added? I gripped my sandwich and gazed at them. This is why the Athenians put Socrates to death, I thought.

For days I brooded about Andrew Jackson, defending him against the swarm of "whys." Actually, I had never quite understood the war against the bank, and I certainly didn't find it interesting. But if I let go of Jackson, what about Monroe or Buchanan or anyone or any event that I had spent a full year reading about in those sixty monographs for my prelim exams? The intellectual ground beneath me grew perilously slippery. Or I should say, positively slippery. I had reached my teachable moment.

I found the solution in Don Oliver's social studies "curriculum for teaching public issues." As students read case studies about controversial episodes in the American past, they would grapple with legal and ethical dilemmas and reflect upon social values. Consider the case of Anthony Burns. The nineteen-year-old slave escaped to freedom in Boston in 1853. A year later, he was discovered and, in accordance with the Fugitive Slave Act, arrested. A judge arranged a trial to verify Burns as a runaway and send him back to his owner in Virginia. A crowd of abolitionists stormed the courthouse to free Burns. A deputy U.S. marshal was stabbed to death. President Franklin Pierce sent troops to subdue the protests. On June 2, 1854, Burns was escorted through two lines of troops to the ship that would return him to slavery. These were the facts, but what meanings did students draw from them? Which side are you on? Freedom or the right of property? Obeying the law or law-breaking in the name of a higher law?

Oliver called this a "jurisprudential" approach. Each case study was like a Supreme Court case, presenting an issue that high school "justices" would explore with legal as well as ethical reasoning. This history wasn't facts and dates, that dry, tasteless concoction served to generations of bored students. It was story, controversy, and inquiry. If you justify the American Revolution, do you also justify the Confederate secession sixty years afterwards?

By the end of my job at the School of Education, I had learned who I wanted to be in my classroom. More than teaching history, I would teach students to wrestle with the past. And where would I put this pedagogy into practice? The Woodrow Wilson Foundation was offering the opportunity for new faculty members to teach in black colleges in the south. What luck, to pursue civil rights in the venue where I felt at home, not the street but the classroom. As it happened, I was assigned to the Midwest rather than the south, and to a formerly all-black university that was half-white with the influx of local students. Regardless, I looked forward to teaching at Lincoln University in Jefferson City, Missouri.

***

As I sat in the lobby of the Harvard Faculty Club dining room, waiting for Frank Freidel, I felt awed by the portraits of eminences staring down upon me. The *Frankfurter Allgemeine Zeitung*, the *Manchester Guardian* and other daily newspapers lay on the coffee table. More Ph.D.s and Nobel Prize winners were chatting here than in any room in America. At least I was wearing a jacket and tie.

Freidel greeted me warmly and escorted me to a table. Midway through the chicken and general conversation, he got to the point. "I finished reading your dissertation. Go ahead and polish it up and submit it to a university press. Now let's talk about jobs. This is one of the best years ever for jobs.

Harvard Days

Openings at Bennington, Stanford, maybe Iowa."

"Actually, I want to teach at a black college in Missouri."

"I've taught at schools like that, Peter. Assigning a rudimentary textbook and pounding the stuff in, again and again. It's a dreary business."

This wasn't what I expected from him. "I'll go for a year, and then I'll see how I feel." But he didn't hear me.

"Harvard trains the elite of the historical profession. I hope you'll use your talents and train the next generation."

I felt defensive, a little desperate to make him understand. "I don't want to train grad students or write books. I want to teach."

He laid down his fork. Looked at me with perplexity. "That's interesting," he murmured.

I wanted to explain to him about—

In the middle of writing that sentence, I've had a *déjà vu*. I am sitting on the living room couch in my high school senior year, telling my father I'm rejecting his kindhearted wish for me and will withdraw my Harvard application. Nine years later, I was leaving Harvard and—yes, now I recognize the parallel for the first time—I was rejecting the kindhearted advice of my fatherly adviser. Bookends to this chapter of my life. Memoir reveals the plotline that memory preserves but doesn't understand.

***

Personal Histories

"Welcome, O life!" Stephen Daedalus exclaims at the end of James Joyce's *Portrait of the Artist as a Young Man*. "I go to encounter for the millionth time the reality of experience and to forge in the smithy of my soul the uncreated conscience of my race."

In June 1965, my colleagues at the School of Education stage a going-away luncheon for me. Lavish sandwiches and salads, a cake, and boisterous toasts. "Good luck finding your way to Missouri." "Don't drink the water." "Did you get your malaria shots?" I smile patiently and am all the more certain it's time to leave Harvard.

A month later, Jeanette and I head west in our new Chevy with two-month-old Benjamin asleep in his crib in the back seat.

1   Matthew Battles, *Widener: Biography of a Library*, (Cambridge, MA: Harvard University Press, 2004), 158-59; Battles, *Library: An Unquiet History* (New York: W.W. Norton, 2003), 15.
2   Wolfe, *Of Time and the River: A Legend of Man's Hunger in His Youth* (NY: Charles Scribner's Sons, 1935), 91.
3   Fitzgerald quoted in Nancy Milford, *Zelda: A Biography* (New York: Avon, 1970), 320
4   Dos Passos to Arthur K. McComb, August 26, 1916, quoted in Melvin Landsberg, *Dos Passos' Path to U.S.A. : A Political Biography, 1912-1936* (Boulder, CO: Associated University Press, 1972,) 48; and Dos Passos, Notebook, Aug. 26, 1917, reprinted in Introduction to Dos Passos, *One Man's Initiation, 1917: A Novel* (Ithaca, NY: Cornell University Press, 1969), 22.

Chapter 6

Reckless Days

Lincoln University

1965-1967

In the thick heat of a Missouri August afternoon in 1965, we parked our Chevy in the driveway at 1506 Notre Dame St. in Jefferson City. The two-bedroom brick ranch house lay low to the ground, unprotected against the sun. As Jeanette carried four-month-old Benjamin (then called "Jamie") indoors, I walked around our new home, rented unseen. Past the carport, I stood in the back yard and looked out over a wire fence toward a golf course green. The yard was big enough for a game of catch some day with Jamie, if we stayed here that long. In the meantime, the clothesline would be handy for diapers. Halfway along the rear of the house, the ground sloped down to make room for the basement where I would set up my study. Trudging through briars, coming full circle past the picture window, I gazed down the driveway toward the mailbox with its red flag. That red flag was like an exclamation point to it all. *I'm a grownup now!* I thought. With this suburban house in the middle of America, with a new baby and an assistant professorship, I've stepped into adulthood.

As I write this memoir a half-century later, I know I was putting on the trappings of maturity, putting on a performance. Even at the time I knew, although I strenuously pushed away the knowing, like swallowing a cough that would interrupt one of my lectures. I bestow a sympathetic smile upon that pretentious young me.

But as he rushes onward in the months ahead, this twenty-five-year-old white newcomer in a mostly black university and a conservative town, he begins to trouble me. *Slow down*, I mutter as I turn the next page in his journal, unfold the next letter in the file. *Pause to reflect.* Yet on he goes, speeding past warning signs, jostling bystanders.

This is not the story I expected to tell. I'd imagined a narrative of what I accomplished, not of who I was, or thought I was. Yes, my adventure in Jefferson City was passionate and exciting, rich with conflict, as a coming-of-age story should be. But of all the many roles I would try on in the next two years, grownup was the one I understood least.

***

My first impression of the university was somewhat bewildering. "I felt like Secretary of State Dean Rusk or the Shah of Massachusetts or something," I wrote in my journal, "as I encountered myself in reputation as 'Doctor Filene, who has come out here from Harvard and Swarthmore.' Particularly because of the 'Doctor' I found myself shaking hands and shaking my head at the same time, while murmuring some Jimmy Stewart-like remark such as 'Just call me Mister.'"[1]

Lincoln University seal

I went to Lincoln on a mission. The Woodrow Wilson Foundation was sponsoring me and two dozen other so-called Teaching Interns to work at historically black Southern colleges, where we would help talented students apply to the best graduate schools. As it happened, Lincoln was in the Midwest and by then the two-thousand student body was only half-black. Local white students, attracted by the $75 tuition rate, were commuting from home. Fraternities, sports teams, and the band were black. White students ate sack lunches or drove to hamburger stands, while black students ate in the cafeteria. "White by day, Black by night," people said. But my essential purpose remained the same: to rescue talented black students.

The obstacles were obvious. "Lincoln is in bad shape and getting worse," I reported to Bill and Elie, our best friends from Harvard days. Half the students held jobs, working twenty or thirty hours a week. Two-thirds of freshmen were in remedial English courses. Because they could register as late as a week after classes began, 125 were trying to learn Western Civilization in a room with sixty-five seats. In desperation, the history department chair even asked Jeanette to teach two sections. After all, she had majored in history in college, hadn't she, and earned a master's in education at Harvard? It was a preposterous notion, teaching a new course on a day's notice while raising an infant—a poignant sign of the state of things at Lincoln. Jeanette politely declined.[2]

Everyone greeted me with wide smiles and earnest handshakes and unsettling well-wishes. "Let's hope you last a year here," they said. "This place is anti-intellectual. Most students are apathetic. Worse, they resent anyone who reads an unassigned book or who tries to get good grades and thereby raises the curve."

Once upon a time, before the civil rights movement, before white colleges had begun luring the best black students and professors, Lincoln had been known as "the black Harvard of the West." Many of the faculty from those days were still at work, including eminent scholars who had made their way in a Negro academic universe alongside the white one.[3] Oliver C. Cox, for example, University of Chicago Ph.D., an influential Marxist sociologist. And Lorenzo Greene, Ph.D. from Columbia in 1942, author of a pioneering book on *The Negro in Colonial New England*. They were the "Doctors," by now a minority among the "Misters and Misses" on the faculty. In any case, they all labored under a teaching load of five courses, which meant preparing fifteen lectures a week for hundreds of ill-prepared students and grading numbingly hundreds of exams. Forget about scholarly research. After 1942, Dr. Greene would co-author only one other book before his death at age eighty-eight.

I was on a mission but determined not to be the deplorable type of missionary—the ones who swarmed across Africa and Asia contemptuously pushing aside native culture. I wanted to share the gifts I'd acquired in my privileged elite schooling. Put on a coat and tie, I told myself, and settle discreetly into your job. Like it or not, though, I was conspicuous. At the opening convocation, the Dean asked the audience to withhold applause as he introduced each new faculty member. But after he recited my pedigree, people clapped loudly and long. My face went hot with embarrassment and, I must admit, pleasure. At Harvard I ran in the middle of the pack. Here I was a celebrity.

Down the hill from Lincoln's century-old red brick buildings, past the crescent of houses that formed the black ghetto, lay Jeff City. If I was a newcomer on campus, I felt altogether foreign as I walked around town. There was one spot of grandeur. The dome of the enormous neoclassical State Capitol Building rose high above the bluffs of the Missouri River. In its shadow, the 30,000 residents worked and shopped on Main Street among a motley collection of brick and clapboard two-story buildings: Woolworths, a few restaurants, a hardware store, one movie theater playing *The Sound of Music* (plus two drive-ins outside town). The Sunday *New York Times* was delivered to the drugstore on Monday afternoons. My sigh turned into a groan when I stepped into the Freedom Bookstore. The shelves were stocked with books by Barry Goldwater (*Conscience of a Conservative*), Billy James Hargis (*Communist America. . . Must it be?*)*,* John Stormer (*None Dare Call It Treason)* and other rightwing authors. "I feel light years away" from home, I told my journal. Painfully far from the Brattle Theater with its Ingmar Bergman films and the Grolier Bookshop crowded with poetry books, poetry magazines, poetry broadsides.[4]

If I had any doubts of my foreignness, I read an editorial in the *Jefferson City News and Tribune*. Local Anti-Poverty Committees may become "the nuclei in a revolutionary struggle" more dangerous than Civil Rights demonstrations, the editors warned, "building a base among the slum-dwellers, the post-school age dropouts, and the permanently delinquent. The U.S. public should know that the most extremist of ideas have taken root in the minds of a new leftwing intelligentsia."

It was August 1965. Watts, the black ghetto in Los Angeles, had just erupted in six days and nights of protest, firefights, and looting, three thousand arrests and thirty-four deaths. On "Bloody Sunday" in March, state troopers in Selma, Alabama, had attacked 500 unarmed civil rights marchers with billy clubs and tear gas. In response, President Lyndon Johnson stood in the House of Representatives urging passage of the Voting Rights Act. "Their cause must be our cause too," he proclaimed. "Because it is not just Negroes, but really it is all of us, who must overcome the crippling legacy of bigotry and injustice."

I was eager to enter my classroom and perform my role in the cause. Fortunately, I had two guides: Dr. Miller, the black chairman of the history and government department, and Pete Kellogg, the Wilson Teaching Fellow who had arrived a year before me.

Dr. Miller wrapped himself in gruff, blunt pronouncements. "Maybe eight or nine of the ninety faculty are any good," he growled. "Only one-third of these students deserve to be in college." He was the son of a manual laborer, went to the University of Pennsylvania in the depths of the Great Depression, taught for eight years before earning a Ph.D. at Penn in 1942 and coming to Lincoln. He was the boss, enthroned in his creaky wooden desk chair in his dusty, disorderly office. I always called him "Dr. Miller." He had fought like hell with the president and the dean to hire Woodrow Wilson Interns and then to establish the honors program as a precious oasis in the intellectual desert. If we got into trouble, we could turn to him as the ardent protector of "my two Peters."[5]

Pete Kellogg was Dr. Miller's counterpart, light to his dark, and I don't mean just his white skin. He was twenty-six-years old, on leave from Northwestern University, where he planned to return in 1966 to finish his dissertation. I liked him immediately; everybody did. He was upbeat, warm and smart. During his first year, he had not only founded the honors program, but launched a history club featuring lectures and book discussions. A handful of students, those with exceptional aspirations or discontents, gathered at his apartment for heated late-night discussions and cold beer. In the wake of "Bloody Sunday" in Selma, they and Pete had raised $1300, rented a bus, and driven with sixteen faculty and students to join the demonstrators. Lincoln had been the hardest year of his life, he told me, and the most gratifying.

"Pete has broken the path," I told my journal, "which I hope to follow in some fashion or another."

The two of us were a terrific team. We interviewed dozens of would-be honors students and selected the best twenty—almost all of them, to our regret, white. These freshmen would be taking the so-called Colloquium seminar that Pete and I had put together during the summer through a giddy exchange of letters and phone calls. "The Good Life," we titled it. Like a classical symphony, the Colloquium had three movements: man and a state of nature; man and society; man and morality. The assigned books pranced across centuries and disciplines. *Lord of the Flies*; *Brave New World*; Plato's *Republic*; *The Communist Manifesto*; Dickens's *Hard Times* and Arthur Miller's *Crucible* followed by Camus' *Plague*; Malraux's acerbic novel, *Man's Fate*. How grandiose, foolhardy and grim! How exciting! The Colloquium was an unwieldy package but, amazingly, it held together—Pete and I held it together—through fourteen weeks of twenty boys and girls tossing it back and forth.

Every Tuesday afternoon, the ten students in my section gathered for three hours. "Some of them are really sharp, one is a silly blonde thing, two boys are just boys," I told Bill and Elie. "But all are earnest, committed to this business of thinking and learning. The week on *Lord of the Flies* went superbly: for three hours we were discussing symbolism, human nature, freedom, war, etc." "It's a razzle dazzle affair," I wrote my parents, "but the kids seem to be enjoying it." Midway through an intense discussion of *Man's Fate*, I proposed a fifteen-minute break. "Not yet," they protested. "First, what **is** the fate?" This was the kind of engagement a teacher dreams of.[6]

On Monday, Wednesday and Friday mornings, I faced the real test of my teaching skills: the seventy-nine students in the introductory course, Columbus to the Civil War. As a fledgling Teaching Fellow at Harvard, I had scornfully dismissed the dean's advice, "Don't worry. Just imitate your best teachers." But now I was worried. I decided to blend the best of what I'd taken from graduate school: one part Bernard Bailyn's elegant lectures on colonial history; one part Don Oliver's case studies containing legal and moral quandaries. Twice a week, I delivered simplified Bailynesque interpretations of Puritan theology, Bacon's Rebellion, mercantilism. On Fridays, I asked the students to serve on the jury at the Salem witchcraft trial or decide whether the Boston Massacre was really the Boston Riot. The pace was dizzying, but at midterm we seemed to be doing fine. "The students here are the friendliest and most open I have ever known," I reported to some old acquaintances.[7] Then came the reckoning.

"It's been a rough week," I lamented in my journal in October. One-fourth of the students, as many white as black, had flunked the first exam. After a high-school diet of short-answer tests, they were bewildered by my essay questions. Three or four pages of short answers didn't add up to an interpretation. "I assume a level of complexity and at this point do not know any way to begin from a simpler level." I didn't know how and, arrogantly, I didn't want to try. "I'm interested in complexity. Any other kind of history neither interests me nor makes sense to me. But most of the kids apparently cannot attain my level. In short, can I communicate to them? Or at what cost?"[8]

Underneath that coat and tie and that Ivy League halo, I was a novice teacher, making the mistake novices make. Fresh out of graduate school, I had forgotten the perspective of ordinary undergraduates. I assumed they would be interested in the esoteric topics that engrossed professional historians. Alas, Puritanism was for my students like what photosynthesis had been for me: words on the blackboard. Instead of abstractions, my students needed narratives—flesh-and-blood characters, actions, colorful details—in order to imagine the past. Easy for me now to recognize my error; unlikely for me back then.

I was walking down the hallway with Mary Savage, an amiable English teacher who had been at Lincoln for decades. "I just graded the midterm exam," I said, "and would you believe it? One-fourth of the kids flunked."

"Oh, I'm sorry," she said. "Yes, I know it can be difficult starting out."

"Thanks, Mary." I felt bolstered by her sympathy.

But then she added, "I hope you figure out what you did wrong."

I jerked to a stop. What *I* did wrong?

I wish I could report that I heeded Mary's advice. But that called for a radically alternative mindset. I would have had to acknowledge that I was only as successful a teacher as my students succeeded in learning. To some extent, professor and student together earn an A or an F. Years later, I came to understand that teaching and learning are halves of a symbiotic process—the First Commandment of pedagogy. But people don't change their minds so easily. The American colonists suffered fifteen years of taxes and Redcoats before they declared revolution, and even then one-third stayed loyal to the Crown. I would evolve slowly.

Meanwhile, I felt stymied. According to one student's essay, "John Adams would sink into mediocracy, false illusionment, and every day drabness." Another student told me he was unsure whether America was rebelling against England in 1776 or the other way around. When Anna, one of the flunked students, came to office hours for help, I was confused by her confusion about the Puritans' settlement in New England. Whatever I said didn't clear up her muddle. After twenty minutes I was about to give up when suddenly I realized, *oh my god, she thinks New England was England in some later time*. Such was the ignorance I was contending with.[9]

If only I had recognized my own ignorance of how my whiteness was blinding me to my black students' perspective

***

As Woodrow Wilson Interns, Pete and I had a reduced teaching load, nine hours instead of fifteen, but that was heavy enough. Colloquium, survey course, and American Foreign

Policy. Weekday mornings, I sprinted from class to office hours and lunch in cafeteria or lunch at home; afternoons were filled with Honors Committee meeting or Colloquium or, Wednesdays, childcare or library research; evenings at home to watch Walter Cronkite with Jamie while Jeanette made dinner (or dinner at 9:00 on Mondays after my Foreign Policy seminar) and finally down to the basement to grade quizzes and prepare tomorrow's lecture. Saturday afternoons I watched Jamie while Jeanette enjoyed time off; Saturday evenings we went out to dinner or a party or an occasional school dance. Sundays I was back in the basement.[10]

Such tireless energy! No wonder I didn't engage in grownup self-reflection and assess consequences. At best, I made judgments on the run. And yet, as if teacher, husband and father weren't enough, I chose to add yet another role. "Agitator," that's what I called it with a certain bravado. Knowing what lies ahead, I wish I could have sounded an alert to that agitator, but he wouldn't have listened. Perhaps celebrity had rendered him a little reckless.

It began at a meeting of the Presbyterian Conference on Religion and Race, which I attended to learn something about the Jeff City community. I sat beside Nate Burger, a young black teacher at the state prison and husband of Magalene, a literature professor. Nate was soft-spoken, earnest, eager to tell me his story. With two young kids, he and Magalene were looking to buy a house outside the ghetto surrounding the campus, but they were having no luck with the realtors. I jumped at the opportunity to use the training I had received, not at Harvard but with the Boston Congress of Racial Equality. Do you want to take part in a test to prove racial discrimination, I asked Nate? Got nothing to lose, he said. The next weekend, Nate and Tom Byers, a young black history teacher, applied for houses in a white neighborhood; then I followed up with the same credentials. After visiting three realtors, the results were flagrant: seventeen houses offered to me, one to Nate, none to Tom. The sole exception was a house on Fairmount Boulevard, priced at $21,000 for Nate, $13,500 a half-hour later for me.

Suddenly, unexpectedly, I had extended my mission beyond the campus. During September and October, I organized a strategy session at the home of Nate and his pretty wife Magalene, including Pete, Tom Byers, Dr. Greene and other black faculty. State law didn't cover housing. So we decided to gather community support with a petition campaign, then confront the board of realtors, and ultimately present a formal complaint to the city human rights commission. The Ad Hoc Committee for Fair Housing, we called ourselves. With business done, people began arriving, beer and bourbon appeared, music and dancing filled Nate and Magalene's living room, and I finally went home to my sleeping wife at midnight. "I have little hope [of fair housing]," I wrote a college classmate, "but I'm having a lot of fun."[11]

During the next month, I sat down and talked with officials across town: at the power and light company, the phone company, a bank, and the Chamber of Commerce. At the Immaculate Conception Catholic Church, I spent a memorable hour with the Rev. Monsignor discussing racial discrimination, then debating whether or not the world reflected God's intent. Everyone was polite and noncommittal. Racism is wrong, they agreed, but time will take care of it.

During my Harvard years, I had neatly compartmentalized my incongruent roles, scholar and protestor. Two months after I arrived at Lincoln, they overlapped. My off-campus agitation splashed back up the hill onto campus and I found myself wading into an academic ruckus. It began promisingly at a faculty meeting. The Ad Hoc Committee presented the fair-housing petition, a majority of professors voted in favor, and Dean Chapman agreed to authorize our victory with his signature. By morning, however, the dean had second thoughts. President Dawson's signature would add weight to the petition, he believed, and I was the person who should request it. I don't remember whether I felt honored or anxious, or if I had any suspicion of being used, but off I went to the president's office.

Earl Dawson was sixty-two years old, a light-skinned Negro with neatly cropped white hair. He had earned a Ph.D. in education from the University of Kansas back in 1942 and gone on to various administrative positions at Lincoln.[12] Seated behind his desk, he seemed too small for his large, wood-paneled office. He listened courteously as I explained my errand. Then, speaking softly, so that I had to lean toward him, he said the issue was not whether he would sign. The faculty had no right to take such action in the first place.

"What we are facing is now no longer simply a question of housing discrimination," I told my journal, "but faculty rights vs. Presidential dictatorship. My instinct, naturally is for confrontation." To my surprise, the faculty agreed. They reaffirmed their support of the petition and sent it back to the president with a strong letter. Back came an equally strong letter, tinged with anger. Senior faculty members, said President Dawson, should have known better than to go beyond their jurisdiction and endanger the university with political action.[13]

Now what? Nothing. There the counterpunching ended, with the petition in limbo. If the fair-housing campaign progressed, it would do so without University support.

But I found other agitation to stir up. Students, at least some of the black students who ate dinner and slept on campus after the white students went home, seethed with discontent. The washing machines in the dorms were closed off at 10:00 p.m., they complained, and half of them didn't work anyway. The TV set in the lounge was broken. You had to spread butter on your bread with forks because there wasn't enough silverware in the cafeteria. The dean stopped guys in the hall and told them to shave off their beards and tuck in their shirts. At the first meeting of the history club, I reported to Bill and Elie, "students launched into a wild vituperative free-for-all about the Uncle Tom president, the arbitrary rules, etc. etc." Alas, I said, it was all talk and no action. The most these dissidents proposed was new washing machines and replacement of the tattered American flag on the main building. "So I have decided to take on the role of radical," I concluded, and thereby open up a path for moderates who would "get something done."[14]

For the time being, though, it remained all talk, by them and by me—a kind of counterpoint to my Bailyn-derived lectures about colonists' speeches and petitions against the Navigation Acts. Business as usual prevailed on campus. The fair-housing campaign in town was moving glacially, if at all. I felt increasingly impatient.[15] One evening, Jeanette cautioned me: Don't jeopardize your effectiveness by trying to reform Lincoln from top to bottom. I resisted her at first, unwilling to slow down and be pragmatic, but in the end, reluctantly, I agreed.[16] As the Midwest cold and snow settled in, I went studiously about my business.

***

And I had unexpected duties at home. In December,

Benjamin and Jeanette Filene, 1966

Jeanette learned she was pregnant. Delightedly, we mused about how Jamie would greet a little brother or, even better, a little sister. But then came some bleeding, and the doctor ordered her to stay in bed. If I felt clumsy as a teacher, I felt more so as a househusband. For five days I was in charge of Jamie, of shopping, of preparing meals, so many unfamiliar tasks while grading seventy-nine book reviews, and sadly, all in vain. A pregnancy test came out negative; the baby was dead. This happens often, the doctor assured us; Mother Nature's way of dealing with a problem. Try again and have better luck. A few days later, I drove her to the hospital for the miscarriage. We exchanged gifts at a lively Christmas party with a dozen of our new friends, but we felt heavy with grief. At midnight New York time on New Year's Eve, we drank a glass of wine, kissed, and declared our love for each other. [17] "I'm certainly glad to rid myself of the last two weeks," I wrote in my journal as I set to work writing lectures, editing a book of readings, and best of all, relishing the news that Harvard Press would publish my dissertation. An author! I was going to be an author!

I did better as a father than a husband. In my journal and letters I celebrated each of Jamie's latest achievements.

> January 1966: He has his third tooth, sits alone, crawls clumsily, and smiles incessantly. He's a nice son.
>
> March: Jamie is cuter every day, especially with his new comradely smile. He is now enthusiastically practicing his latest talent: sitting down from a standing position.
>
> September: He chews pebbles, says 'cat,' and is a splendid son.
>
> October: He tugs at our hands, pulls us to the record player, listens in delight to Beatles or a Bach cantata and goes into his inimitable dance: head nod, or shoulder heave, or shuffleshuffle, or simply wheel around in a circle.[18]

Jeanette, meanwhile, gets sporadic attention in my letters and journals, and without the gusto I devoted to Jamie. Of course that is the typical emotional economy in families. Baby consumes a lion's share of the energy and delight. In holiday photographs, husband and wife stand wider and wider apart at the edges of their growing family. Nevertheless, I could have used some lessons in husbandry.

March, 1966: Jeanette is busy with Jamie from dawn (literally) till dusk or more. But she also serves as Madame Treasurer of the new chapter of the League of Women Voters.

Benjamin and Peter Filene, 1966

April: Jeanette is enjoying herself very much as a mother, somewhat less so as a housewife and citizen of Jeff City. She is a bit isolated, mentally as well as physically.

August: Jeanette is content. She's taking another course and playing with her new vacuum cleaner.

October: Jeanette is enjoying drama course and piling up tin cans for Jamie to knock down. She is generally having a nice life.[19]

Tin cans piled up and knocked down, I said. Playing with the vacuum cleaner, I said. What did Jeanette say? In 1966 I agitated for the rights of Negroes and students, but I hadn't yet been confronted by the women's liberation movement.

***

When classes began in January, I shrugged off Jeanette's caution and happily resumed my role as agitator-radical. Joe Gentry, one of my students, had been discovered one night in a motel with his girlfriend. For this violation of college rules, the personnel committee sentenced him to social probation. I no longer know what that entailed—presumably a semester-long banishment from dances, movies and such. But President Dawson felt the punishment wasn't severe enough; he decreed a semester's suspension. This was hardly equivalent to British troops gunning down Bostonians in the so-called massacre, but I exploded with outrage. In a letter to Dawson, I denounced his infringement of student rights. I also sent the letter to the student newspaper, calling upon students and faculty to consider changing the regulations of student conduct. One girl stopped me in the hall. "I agree with you 200 percent, 100 for me, 100 for you."

Dawson, on the other hand, wrote to me with "astonishment" that I had intervened. Of course he believed in freedom of speech, but that was not the issue. My behavior, that was the issue. By not going through proper channels for changing university regulations, I had violated "professionality." And by sending my letter to the newspaper, I had appealed to the "immature minds" of students. Take this incident as a lesson about my responsibilities.

"Now I am *really* infuriated—and incredulous," I exclaimed in my journal. "Apparently he believes that free speech and open criticism are not permitted on campus, by students or faculty."[20] Freedom versus dictatorship; right versus wrong; none of the ambiguity of Don Oliver's case studies. As for Dawson himself, I disparaged him as "a sixty-two-year-old, quite incompetent, Uncle Tom."[21]

"I'm having a wonderful time," I blithely announced in my journal.[22] Too wonderful to notice a glaring discrepancy. I was agitating on behalf of students, yet I defined their cause in my terms, not theirs. Instead of washing machines, cafeteria silverware and sex, I advocated abstract principles of rights and free speech. What a telling coincidence that Bernard Bailyn wrote about *The Ideological Origins*, not the material causes, *of the American Revolution*. Whether as teacher or agitator, I wasn't fully listening to my students.

***

Meanwhile, the Ad Hoc Committee pushed onward—or were we treading water? We staged more tests of realtors. Final score: 40 to 5, forty houses offered to white applicants, five unsuitable houses to Negroes. We held public hearings where, predictably, Nate Burger, Dr. Greene and other black citizens cited discrimination and bankers and realtors excused it. I wasn't prepared, though, for Ray Brummet's testimony. He'd done some investigating, Brummet said, and he'd discovered that the Woodrow Wilson Foundation was "sprinkled with leftist elements," including Alger Hiss, that Communist agent in the State Department. Brummet pointed at Pete Kellogg and me. Those Wilson interns are the only white members of the committee, he said, and they'd come to Jeff City to stir up trouble. I nearly laughed out loud at this echo of McCarthyism ten years after McCarthy's death. It was ridiculous, but I also found it a little intoxicating to be cast as a Communist agent.[23]

Our campaign made unexpected progress. In June, 1966, the mayor appointed a committee of one hundred people (including me as second vice-chairman) to study the problem of racial discrimination and, by November 1, to recommend solutions.[24]

And then what happened? And then fair housing vanishes from my journal and letters. Not a word. Which is to say, I vanished as agitator-teacher in the civic arena. I don't remember whether the mayor adopted our recommendation or stashed it in a drawer, but ultimately it didn't matter. Two years later, the federal government would take over. Title VIII of the 1968 Civil Rights Act required equal access to fair housing for all Americans.[25]

I left the civic arena because I was swept up again in a tempest on campus. It began with a student's small handwritten cardboard sign.

***

When Jeanette and I moved from Cambridge to Jeff City, we turned the cultural clock back two or three years— History Central Time. Here the battle for civil rights was for integration and understanding between the races. Black and white together, we shall overcome. But Stokely Carmichael, leader of the Student Nonviolent Coordinating Committee (SNCC) was preaching Black Power and black consciousness.

"Integration is an insidious subterfuge when initiated by blacks alone."[26] SNCC and CORE, the organization in which I had been initiated into the Movement, told white members to get out and combat the racism of their own people.

Students at Lincoln were scrambling to keep up with these developments, and so was I. At a History Club symposium in the spring of 1966 on "Which Way to Freedom for the Negro?" the first two panelists, both of them black, endorsed integration. The next two indicted "Toms" and "crackers," especially "that cracker in the White House." Colored people around the world, they proclaimed, are rising up against white imperialist oppression. "That's right," the crowd shouted, "You tell 'em, baby." I was astounded, unsettled by the taunts and raucous laughter. This was not the Lincoln I knew, or thought I knew. Most of the Negro students, I believed, were not stoking black consciousness or separatism. Like Nate and Magalene Burger, they wanted to enjoy the rights and opportunities of white middle-class Americans. I could have used Pete Kellogg's counsel. He had socialized with radical black students and understood their dissidence, but Pete had returned to Northwestern.[27]

Come hear Jennifer Lawson speak about Black Power. That was the handwritten sign Bob Bass wore on his shirt while doing his work-study job in the library. Jennifer Lawson was a SNCC field secretary in Alabama whom the History Club had invited to talk at Lincoln. For the head librarian, Dr. A.J. Marshall, she represented chaos. "Either you take off that sign," he told Bass, "or you don't work for me." Bass refused and Marshall fired him. I encouraged Bass to take his case to the Student Government Association, and as sponsor of the History Club I made sure to attend the hearing. Dr. Marshall testified he had the right to hire and fire his employees. In any case, he said, the invitation to Jennifer Lawson violated proper procedures. I couldn't restrain myself. "Do you agree with Dr. Marshall?" I asked the SGA president. Two days later, I received a letter from President Dawson reprimanding me for unprofessional conduct by showing up a colleague. Indignantly, I made an appointment to reply.[28]

As I accompany that young version of myself to Dawson's doorstep, I want to put my hand on his shoulder and say, *Stop and think! Understand that he's shackled by sixty years of being a Negro in America. Understand that he must bow to the state legislators downtown who dole out the meager appropriations for his university. Easy for you, Doctor from Harvard, to make a righteous protest.*

But that young white man strode in and I cringe, knowing what happened next.

I don't advocate Black Power, I said, but I do advocate students' right to hear Jennifer Lawson.

SNCC's program is misguided and dangerous, the president replied; not the sort of ideas for students' immature minds.

You're denying freedom of speech, I declared. Firing Bob Bass was unjust.

Then Dawson held out his hand. "Dr. Filene, look at the color of this skin. You're white, you don't understand what it means to be a Negro. Students have to learn to do things even if they don't want to. They're going to face injustices in life, and they have to learn to do so."

I left his office with the same fury and certainty I had carried into it. "Here are people who don't understand the principle of free speech," I told friends. "And here is Uncle

Tomism, brainwashing so thorough that the Negroes themselves can't even recognize it any more. There are many splendid exceptions, including Dr. Miller, who has supported me 100 percent throughout. But not enough to really give me the feeling Lincoln can emerge from its post-slave cocoon in the near future—certainly not until Dawson retires. So I'm more than ever convinced it's time to go. I got a letter from Stony Brook University on Long Island..."[29]

Yes, midway through my second year, furtive thoughts of departure had begun flickering in my mind. Emigration to one of those elite campuses my Harvard adviser had urged me to apply to. A culturally richer environment, as Jeanette astutely said, where it wouldn't be so easy to be important. Where I would have time to write. My forthcoming book would be my passport. Dr. Miller begged me to stay a third year. I felt like a traitor to him, to the larger cause, and yet I hungered for what I used to have.[30]

***

At the same time, though, I was beginning to do a better job of teaching. Good teachers leave a class asking themselves what went right, what went wrong. In the second semester, I had felt secure enough to stop blaming students for my wrongdoing. And self-critical enough to ask for help from Pete and Jeanette. Hold in mind the hierarchy of cognitive skills, they said—from low-level recitation up the steps to complex interpretation. Ask students to do simpler skills before more difficult ones. Also, they suggested, measure my success by assigning a quick quiz at the start of class and repeating it at the end of class. The result was equivocal. Seventeen students improved, ten stayed the same, four decreased. As one student was leaving class, she said she was more confused than before. Maybe I should stop teaching, I joked. "Oh no, Dr. Filene, you're the best teacher I've had."[31]

I was doing one thing right. I was enthusiastic. Every Monday, Wednesday and Friday I strode into the classroom, opened my briefcase, chalked names and dates on the blackboard, and welcomed my students with a smile. "I am learning, by trial and woeful error, how to teach."

I was also beginning to talk less and listen more—during class, and especially during office hours.

Pat Bonner, a student from Jamaica, explained she didn't write the book review because she disliked reading books about the past. I said my wife was fascinated with the Middle Ages. Pat made a face. "That era was backward." To change the subject, I asked which ten things she would take if sentenced to a desert island? Food, she said, a sun hat, water, and a radio. "No books?" I asked. She laughed. "People. I'd bring people."

Max Trujillo, the burly forty-five-year-old student in my foreign policy class, tipped his chair back and recounted his life story. The son of a coal miner. As a teenager, worked in New Deal Civilian Conservation Corps. Then twenty-six years in the Army. Disgusted with the Army and the Vietnam war. Working on a master's degree in education.

Magalene Burger came by again after teaching her English class. She talked about the problems that fathers face in Negro families, and about her own struggles to be a good teacher while also taking care of Chip and Hank and the house. Nate would be at work tomorrow evening. Did I want to take her to a party for a visiting English professor?

"Every conversation seems to teach me something," I wrote in my journal. "I come home exhausted but fascinated."[32]

***

On Saturday afternoon, the phone rang. Cancel your visit next weekend, my father said. Mother is ill. Then she spoke, sounding shaky, almost a stranger's voice. Days later, my father phoned again. Mother was in the hospital. A stroke. Her right side paralyzed. I hung up and couldn't breathe, dread clogging my throat. Off we flew to New York, Ozark Air propeller plane to Lambert St. Louis and jet to LaGuardia, our little family of three. When I arrived at Mount Sinai Hospital, I could barely register the sight of my mother lying on the bed amid tubes and blinking machines. She spoke slowly, struggling to find the right word, lapsing into German. She kept asking me where she was. With her usual will power, she tried to write with her left hand, square and clumsy letters. "I have not fully absorbed the fact of the way she is. I look at her as someone different (temporarily) from the woman I called Mother."[33]

***

Teacher, agitator, father and husband, son. My roles were multiplying, overlapping, competing with each another.

> May 1966: Too much talk, problems, personal tensions, red tape, etc. I want to retreat to my study, open a book. I want to rescue my individuality, return to the art studio of the mind. I don't have time for myself. I feel emotionally inadequate.[34]

It was a call for help, but I kept it inside my journal and I was too confused to help myself. More to the point, I had only the dimmest sense of who that self might be.

Personal Histories

***

When Jennifer Lawson arrived, she brought with her the wind of revolt. The twenty-year-old SNCC worker would have attracted attention simply because of her Afro, unique at Lincoln. But after the dean refused to let her speak on campus, she seemed excitingly dangerous. The History Club reserved a dingy community center for the shoulder-to-shoulder crowd. I had expected Stokely Carmichael's shrill in-your-face style, but Lawson spoke softly—deceptively so. After describing her work in Lowndes County, Alabama, she turned the spotlight on Lincoln. Blacks should beware of white students dominating their university, she said. Blacks and whites can't understand each other. Whites should return to their own communities and "civilize" them. I silently disagreed, of course. I hoped we could lower the barriers between the races, not raise them. Then again, her assertiveness was a refreshing contrast with Dawson's servility. And wasn't I planning to go back to a white university? By the end of her visit, I was feeling confused. "Black power" made more sense than I'd expected.[35]

Weeks later, a handful of black students gathered in my office to say they were putting together an underground newspaper. Call it *Common Sense*, I suggested, thinking of Tom Paine's 1776 pamphlet demanding American independence. But they didn't need advice from their white history professor. A week later, *The Student Liberator* appeared under dormitory doors, in classrooms and latrines. On the front page, a cartoon portrayed a stoop-shouldered man labeled "Dawson" saying, "We don't want troublemakers around here." Inside, an article itemized a myriad of complaints, especially conditions in the cafeteria, and accused the administration of incompetence and tyranny.[36]

Wednesday, April 5, 1967. Jeanette and I are eating dinner, with Jamie in his high chair merrily chewing his green beans or dropping them overboard, when the phone rings. "You've got to come to the cafeteria," a friend says. "A riot's going on."

Ten minutes later I'm there, amid a swirl of hundreds of students carrying signs, *Down with Dawson, We Want Good Food, No More Uncle Tom*. Helmeted policemen with riot sticks stand by calmly. People I don't recognize in suits and ties, long dresses, huddle on the sidelines. I step over food and plates on the floor, glass from broken windows. What the hell happened, I ask my friend?

The annual Headliners Banquet was taking place in the upstairs dining room, she explains. Guests from NBC, *Newsweek*, the Associated Press, were eating prime rib, asparagus à la mornay, and potatoes au gratin. Students down here were eating one greasy spare rib, a slice of bread, and dessert. "I ain't eating no more of this shit," an athlete shouted, and threw his plate on the floor. Other students jumped to their feet, yelling, tossing plates and trays, toppling tables.

As we're talking, a chorus of jeers breaks out. President Dawson has arrived. He stands frozen in the doorway, expressionless, a man in shock. When he tries to address the crowd, he can't make himself heard.[37]

Events during the next week take place at exhilarating speed. *This is what a revolution feels like*, I tell myself.

Wednesday night: Student leaders draft a list of grievances: cafeteria; broken washing machines; housemothers entering rooms without knocking; dress code for girls; censorship of school newspaper. Sixty-four grievances. Ranging from mundane indignities to abstract injustice.

Thursday: Boycott of classes. Dawson tells a student gathering, "I will take the grievances under advisement," and exits to a volley of boos and jeers.

Tom Byers and I and other faculty friends join a thousand students marching downtown, waving to curious townsfolk. Chants of "Black Power" alternate with football cheers. Two hours in the baking heat outside the Capitol Building, and finally the governor's assistant emerges. A legislative committee, he says, will investigate conditions on campus.

Friday: The boycott spreads and now comes my moment. A teach-in. Several hundred kids are sitting on the lawn in afternoon sunshine. Someone introduces me, applause bursts out, and the same thrill ripples through my chest as it did two years ago at the opening convocation.

I haven't prepared a speech, but the words come on their own. "This is a student revolt that will lift oppression from students and faculty. I can speak because I'm leaving in June; other faculty have to protect their jobs. You are taking your destinies into your own hands. For two days you've boycotted classes and you've received more education than during any other two days of the year." They cheer and clap. I point to the kids sitting next to the uprooted "Don't Walk on the Grass" signs. I note that girls are wearing slacks. This meeting, I declare, is taking place without the dean's permission. "Ask why, and listen for the answer, and if the other side doesn't answer, take action to be heard."

That evening, I confer with protest leaders about their meeting tomorrow with the Board of Curators.

Sunday: The Curators promise to deal with the demands and to levy no reprisals.

Reckless Days

Thursday: Dawson agrees to reform conditions in the cafeteria and dorms. But he holds tight to his tyrannical power. Except for abolishing dress codes, the administration will continue to monitor and censor students.[38]

***

A week later, I was talking with a black student about her exam, trying to clarify the meaning of revolution.

"What would a revolutionist do at Lincoln?" I asked.

"Improve the cafeteria," she replied.

"No," I said. "He would oust Dawson."

She looked out the window for a moment. "But I don't want a revolution at Lincoln," she said quietly. "I think things are all right here."[39]

Two years later, after none of the promised reforms were implemented, students would rebel more violently and Dawson would resign.[40] In May 1967, by contrast, the campus returned to peace. "The euphoria is dwindling now," I complained in my journal, "like a balloon that has been put in the corner of a closet and left there several days. Students have been bought off. . . . They are happier, better fed, and again apathetic. But I didn't expect more."

I was also "bitterly disappointed" by my colleagues. So many "seem anxious to hide within silence or routine, pulling the blinders more tightly to the sides of their heads." At a meeting called to approve some of the student demands, they bickered for twenty minutes about whether a looser rule on smoking would deprive the instructor of his classroom sovereignty. Even Dr. Miller had succumbed. The dean had punished Tom Byers by rescinding a grant he had earned. Despite my plea, Dr. Miller refused to intervene. "I'm tired of defending members of my department and the Internship program," he said.

I, in turn, was disgusted with the "incredible apathy and obtuseness."[41]

***

Reading these words, I have the impulse to disown that callow youth, or at least pound some empathy into him. But that would manufacture another me. On second thought, let's grant forgiveness. If he had understood then what I understand now, he wouldn't have been young, passionate, impatient to remake the world from top to bottom. "These have been two of the most educational, important and exciting years of my life. I have done something. I have made a mark."[42] He was arrogant, but arrogance can sometimes accomplish things that prudence doesn't dare. Consider this list.

Creating the Colloquium seminar.

Defending the rights of students and faculty.

Launching the campaign for fair housing.

Ironically, my specific mission as Woodrow Wilson Intern proved least successful. In the end, I steered exactly one student into graduate school—Yale, no less—but she was white and didn't last beyond her first year.

As for internal development, I remained more adolescent than grownup. "I feel circumscribed by my habits and restraints (self-imposed).... Romantically I still expect some big breakthrough somewhere ahead, a sudden release into a bright and breathless realm in which I am and create more than ever before." But that grandiosity fueled my energy and, who knows, inspired some students to imagine beyond their bounds.

Amid all this turbulence there was personal tragedy:

> I've wondered why I have said and written so little about my mother's death. First of all, because I don't want to think about it. . . .
>
> Also because she became someone other than my mother, disappearing a year ago. Death was only the end of departure.
>
> And finally, I must admit, I had been departing from her for a long time. The intimacy was gone some years ago. I don't know why.[43]

This brusque journal entry is all I wrote—short shrift for such an enormous event. Only thirty years later, with the help of psychotherapy, would I gain the courage to grieve the loss of my mother.

***

In January I had visited Chapel Hill to be interviewed for a job at the University of North Carolina. I was wined and dined and offered a salary of $10,000 with a promise of tenure. The history department was eager for a young teacher with a book and Harvard to his name. I had hoped for a job in New England or New York, home territory, but there were no openings. So Jeanette and I agreed: why not try a Southern, mostly white university for a year or two?

Shortly after the student revolt, I spent three days at a historians' convention in Chicago. "I'm breathing enthusiastically the air of professionalism. Inwardly, I still shake my head a bit—my god, I am a genuine historian, part of the guild. I am itchy to resume my other disguise—not as agitator but as scholar."[44]

Disguise? Looking back, that piece of wit hits me in the face. Like many jokes, it says more than the speaker realized. A disguise implies a self underneath. The sad truth is, I was putting on costumes and taking them off, never pausing long enough to observe my naked self. Grownup. Teacher. Husband and father. Agitator. Communist. Son. Scholar.

Quick-change artists are performers who switch within seconds from one costume to the next, dazzling the audience. I won many friends, admirers and enemies, applause and hostility. I occupied a bright spotlight. But I would remain invisible to myself for years to come.

***

Early one warm June morning, we drove past the red mailbox, our family of three, and headed east. I was looking forward to teaching white Carolina students about American history, social justice and racism. The role in which I was happiest, most myself, was in a classroom. That much I knew.

1   Journal, May 11, 1965. For narrative purposes, I have blended two entries: one describing my preliminary visit in the spring, the other after I began teaching.
2   To Bill and Elie Rosenberg, Sept. 29, 1965. All my letters, most of them carbon copies, are in my possession. Likewise, my journal.
3   Shirley McCarther, Donna Davis, and Loyce Caruthers, "A Place Called Homecoming: Memories of Celebration and Tradition by Successful African-American Graduates of Lincoln University in Missouri from 1935 to 1945," The Journal of Educational Foundations: Ann Arbor, 26 (Summer 2012), 7-32.
4   Journal, August 22, 1965.
5   Journal, May 11, 1965.
6   To Parents, Sept. 28, 1965; to Bill and Elie Rosenberg, Sept. 29, 1965.
7   To Frants and Judy Albert, Dec. 17, 1965.
8   Journal, Oct 28, 1965
9   To my parents, Oct. 2, 1966; and to Frants and Judy Albert, Dec. 17, 1965.
10 To my parents, Oct. 2, 1966.
11 Meeting and party in Journal, Oct. 3, 1965. House prices cited in testimony to Mayor's Commission, *News and Tribune,* March 4, 1966; quotation in letter to Lanny Rubin, Oct 24, 1965.
12 Cyntida J. Chapel, *Shifting History, Shifting Mission, Shifting Identity: The Search for Survival at Lincoln University (Jefferson City, Missouri) 1866-1997* (unpub. dissertation, Oklahoma State University, 1997), 369.
13 Journal, Oct. 28, 1965; to my parents, Nov. 22, 1965.
14 To Bill and Elie, Sept. 29, 1965; to Lanny Rubin, Oct. 24, 1965, and April 29, 1965.
15 To my parents, Nov. 22, 1965.
16 Journal, Oct. 3, 1965.
17 Journal, Jan. 1, 1966.
18 Journal entries; and letters to Juan and Martha Hovey, Sept. 3, 1966, and to Bill and Elie Rosenberg, Oct. 29, 1966.
19 To Harvard Project People, March 29, 1966; to Lanny Rubin, April 29, 1966; Journal, Aug 16, 1966; to Bill and Elie Rosenberg, Oct. 28, 1966.
20 Journal, Jan. 23, 1966.
21 To Lanny, April 29, 1966.
22 Journal, Jan. 23, 1966.

23 *Jefferson City News and Tribune,* March 4, 1966; to Jim and Jill Holt, March 4, 1966.
24 To Bob and Kitty Sklar, Aug 25, 1966; to Juan and Martha Hovey, Sept 3, 1966; to my parents, Oct. 2, 1966; to Bill and Elie Rosenberg, October 28, 1966.
25 http://missourilawyershelp.org/lesson-plans/the-fair-housing-act/
https://www.jeffersoncitymo.gov/government/redevelopment_and_grants/fair_housing_information.php
26 Paul Good, "The Meredith March," *New South* (Summer 1966), reprinted in *Reporting Civil Rights, Part Two, American journalism 1963-1973*, (New York: The Library of America, 2003), 504-05.
27 For the symposium and my reaction, see "The Most Segregated Integrated University," an unpublished essay I wrote in August 1967; and Pete Kellogg's letters to me critiquing the essay, Aug. 22 and 25, 1967.
28 To Bill and Elie Rosenberg, Oct. 28, 1966.
29 To Bill and Elie Rosenberg, Oct. 28, 1966.
30 Journal, Aug. 16 and June 19, 1966.
31 Journal, March 18 and April 3, 1966.
32 Journal, April 3, 1966.
33 Journal, June 19, 1966.
34 Journal, May 9 and 27, 1966.
35 To Bill and Elie, Dec. 11, 1966.
36 To Bill and Elie, Dec. 11, 1966.
37 To my father, April 11, 1967.
38 To my father, April 11, 1967; to Bill and Elie Rosenberg, April 30, 1967.
39 Journal, April 23, 1966.
40 Chapel, *Shifting History, Shifting Mission, Shifting Identity,* 388-92.
41 Journal, May 4, 1967.
42 Journal, May 4 and June 10, 1967.
43 Journal, May 4, 1967.
44 To Bill and Elie Rosenberg, April 30, 1967.

Chapter 7

A Letter to my Students

The classroom is my country and you, my college students, are my compatriots. During forty-three years I taught 170 or so courses. All in all, I figure there must be, very approximately, ten thousand of you. A small town.

At first, you inhabited three courses meeting three hours a week, including Tuesday, Thursday, Saturday at 8:00 a.m., god help us. Soon that was reduced to two courses and no Saturdays. The teaching load, that's what professors call it with a grimace. When I told a friend I had written a book on *The Joy of Teaching*, he said "it must be a short book." Okay, teaching wasn't entirely joyful. But without all those lectures to prepare and exams to grade, how would I have met you?

You're still with me, in my mind's eye, hovering between youth and adulthood, although of course you're middle-aged or older, maybe retired, or dare I say dead. I see you in row after row of faces or bent heads, a hundred of you aligned or confined but in any case too many for me to recognize unless you asked or answered questions or came to office hours. More hospitably, I picture you who formed seminar circles, who had names and personalities and even lives you recounted beyond the bounds of "The U.S. since 1945" or "The History of Photography." Best of all, I greet you who sat within arm's reach in my office to confess about your late paper or voice confusion about the Second New Deal, to confer about your honors thesis chapter, or simply, honestly, to converse about living in Spain, racism, feeling inauthentic or, in tears, your parents' divorce—the real stuff.

But even stronger than memory, look here. You spill out of this bulging folder in my filing cabinet, a marvelous assembly addressing me in words you typed, printed out or handwrote on greeting cards, postcards, stationery, and torn sheets of notebook paper, days, years, even decades after your final grade.

I've written memoir essays on certain episodes or themes of my life. But you're far more than an episode or theme. You, my companions through the past fifty years, have been my calling. You're the other half of the dialogue of teaching learning. It's time I wrote a thank you.

***

I began my career teaching a section of what Harvard called General Education A, which aimed to train Freshmen (yes, first-year males) in writing and critical reading. I was training myself a desperate week ahead of them. Teaching is both craft and art, but back then, in the fall of 1961, I concentrated on crafting. It was like playing an instrument for the first time, a matter of notes (wrong and right) rather than melody. I was barely older than the twenty students, which my tweed jacket didn't fully disguise. "Hey," one said as I walked into the classroom, "what do you know about the instructor?" "He's me," was the best I could muster. The first few months I made every mistake in the book. But there was hope. At the end of the first semester, someone handed me a penciled note. "Mr. Filene. We all admired the enthusiasm with which you taught Gen Ed. It could have been a dull, non-benefitting course, but it wasn't. Thank you."

In retrospect, though, I see I was, tentatively and unwittingly, taking small steps toward the kind of pedagogy I aspired to. *Pedagogue* derives from Greek *paidagogus*, slave who supervised children, including taking them to and from school. I vividly remember after-class conversations with Marshall, a shy boy from a town in Georgia. He felt overwhelmed by the crowds and pace of Cambridge, he confided in a soft Southern accent. He was scared to talk in class among his smart-talking prep-school classmates. You're smart enough, I insisted. Over the next few weeks, I asked about Marshall's family, his interests, and one day, on some undefined impulse, took him to The Grolier Bookstore crowded to the ceiling with poetry books. What influence did I have on his future at Harvard? I wish I knew.

Teachers never know the influence we exert, bad or good. Often it's just as well. But sometimes we're happily taken by surprise. In 2017 I received an email with the subject line, *Did you teach Gen Ed A at Harvard in early 1960s?* "This may seem a strange request," Russell Maulitz explained, "but in reading just today in *The New Yorker* about James Baldwin, I thought about—well, it was either you or your doppelganger. I'd love to be in touch."

How in the world do you remember me, I wrote back? Yes, I taught that course and learned far more than I taught.

"Don't be so sure!" Russ replied. "I learned gobs from you. One of my best experiences at Harvard. I'd no idea how young you were, or how green. Just got blown away reading James Baldwin with you and having to react to him. So whenever I read him, or about him, or run into films like *I Am Not Your Negro*, I think of Gen Ed A."

Gobs! "I'm still at heart a teacher," I replied, "and it heartens me to hear I (well, Baldwin) had an effect."

Somehow I had transcended craft and, with James Baldwin's aid, made a difference, an indelible mark. During the next years, I would work on accomplishing that mysterious goal intentionally.

***

At Lincoln University in Jefferson City, Missouri, I continued struggling with the craft. Hardly surprising. First, preparing three different courses from scratch was a sleep-defying feat. And then take into account the students who sat in those courses. They differed drastically from those I had known in my journey through the precious realm of Friends School, Swarthmore and Harvard. Because of limited training in high school, many were ill-prepared for college-level work, as least as I defined college level. Moreover, because of financial necessity, a majority spent twenty or thirty hours a week at jobs. And then there was the difference I was even less prepared to understand: race. Half the students were Black, because Lincoln was a Historically Black College recently desegregated by local whites.

A Letter to my Students

In Gen Ed A, I had needed to learn more than I taught. Russ and his classmates progressed well enough without or despite me. At Lincoln my need to learn was more fraught—intellectually, but also culturally and personally. I tried, zealously I tried to overcome the challenges just as I had always tried in my climb toward my Ph.D. But somehow I kept slip-sliding short of my aspirations. "John Adams would sink into mediocracy, false illusionment, and every day drabness," a student wrote. He might have been describing my view of the class. As things went wrong, I'm chagrined to say I did the classic teacher gambit. When one-third flunked the first exam, instead of asking why my teaching had fallen short, I blamed them. "I'm interested in complexity," I scribbled in my journal. "Any other kind of history neither interests me nor makes sense to me. But most of the kids apparently cannot attain my level."

The "kids" were remarkably forgiving, but then again, they had no choice, did they? Week after week, exam after exam, they struggled to meet my expectations. Finally, after months of impasse, I had to acknowledge the problem might also be partly mine. As a measure of my effectiveness, I assigned a quick, ungraded quiz at the start of class and repeated it at the end of class. The result was wincingly instructive. Seventeen students improved their score, ten stayed the same, four decreased. "I'm more confused than before," one remarked while leaving class. Maybe I should stop teaching, I joked. "Oh no, Dr. Filene, you're the best teacher I've had."

That was kind of her, like my high school baseball coach patting me on the shoulder after I struck out. I was a rookie teacher with a dubious batting average, but at least I was hungry to learn.

Dear Lincoln students, this is a belated thank you for your patience.

Personal Histories

***

After two years, I took a job at the University of North Carolina. In 1967, Chapel Hill was a southern Jefferson City: twenty-some thousand residents in what was still called "the village"; one movie theater; foreign cuisine represented by a Chinese restaurant and a pizza place. It proudly bore the label as a liberal oasis, but desegregation of restaurants and the white high school had taken place only after whites' bitter resistance and the federal Civil Rights Act. Jeanette and I assumed this would be a brief stopover en route north, back to where we came from and belonged. During the first eight or ten years, I read *The New York Times* as my local newspaper.

UNC seemed equally foreign: twenty thousand students, the great majority from small towns across North Carolina along with a 12 percent quota of out-of-staters (all but a hundred, in contrast with Lincoln, white). But in the classroom, my realm, I felt at home. Most students were prepared to do college-level work and I was excited to teach them. That first year—oh, it started off as a beguiling honeymoon. Beyond hitting the correct notes, I began playing the melody and, occasionally, composing my own—in concert with my students.

On paper, the curriculum looked conventional. I taught three courses per semester: a survey allegedly "covering" U.S. history from Columbus to the Civil War; a more modest survey from the Great Depression onwards; and a seminar on a topic of my choice. Two hundred-plus students. Definitely a load. But this was 1967, and current events were arousing their minds and bodies. There was that hopeless war in Vietnam and the dreaded draft. Civil rights and urban riots. Drugs, rock concerts, self-actualization, and in oh so far-out San Francisco, the Summer of Love.

A Letter to my Students

Not just students were aroused; also many young teachers. As part of the tide of newly hired faculty, too many to be housed in the central history department building, I shared an office in a former dormitory at the front edge of campus with free-spirited, politically activist sociologists and historians. Paula Goldsmid taught me feminism. Dick Roman preached socialism. All of us opposed the war and, between classes, enjoyed throwing darts at the face of LBJ on a dartboard. In the Presbyterian Student Center, a chaplain with the deceptively bland name of Harry Smith invited me to brownbag lunches with faculty engaged in innovative teaching. Towny Ludington inducted me into the American Studies program he had founded the previous year—a two-man curriculum that forged a bold, wobbly path across the disciplines of history, literature and art.

These were the multitudes of influences I carried into my classrooms where students awaited me. Professorially, I delivered lectures filled with names, dates and nuanced interpretation. But more to the point of learning, we met in small weekly circles and discussed dramatic case studies. Was the Boston Massacre actually an urban riot? Should northerners have sent escaped slaves back to their masters? In the American Studies seminar, we viewed the past through novels and poetry, autobiographies, paintings and photographs, political narratives.

In 2020, I received this email in my mailbox, a very belated course evaluation from Dave Eason.

> Dr. Filene:
>
> I am now 63 and after a long career in forensic and addiction psychiatry, I now reflect on people that inspired my curiosity and helped grow my success.

> Peter, I grew so much from the multimedia American Studies courses you taught, both exposing me to certain writers as well as developing feminist perspectives. As one example, I still use quotes from the marvelous poetry of Louis Simpson to whom you "turned me on."

By my second semester, though, case studies and multi-genre sources were tame pedagogy. In the survey "From Reconstruction to the Present," my syllabus began with *Freedom Road*, a novel by Howard Fast, a former Communist, and ended with "The Student as Nigger," an essay in the *Los Angeles Free Press*, an underground newpaper. In "Recent U.S. History," after I dutifully led a hundred students through the Great Depression and the 1950s, I planted similar provocations. One week, we argued about Betty Friedan's *Feminine Mystique*. The next week, Stokely Carmichael's *Black Power*. Finally, Norman Mailer's *The American Dream* paired with *The Great Gatsby*. I look back and laugh incredulously at these brazen assignments. They were in keeping with my Converse hightops and new reddish beard. And with asking students to call me Peter.

The crucial question, though, is what did you make of all my efforts? I could measure attendance (steady) and grades (lots of B's and A's). But what about the immeasurable consequences? After you finished writing the final exam, you shook my hand and murmured, "I really enjoyed the class"—the politeness Southerners were trained to give, albeit ending with "Peter" instead of "sir." As I recall, most end-of-course evaluations ranged from positive to enthusiastic. But memory is untrustworthy. Here are two tangible pieces of evidence from my file cabinet.

A Letter to my Students

First, a handwritten note I found taped on my office door after the final exam.

Dear Peter,

I want to thank you <u>before</u> we've all disappeared.

This class has been one of the greatest influences in my life because I am finally having to face the contradictions of tradition vs. reality in myself & those around me. Your style of teaching was essential and effective and I <u>hated</u> to miss a single class.

In sum: thanks for helping me grow.

Sincerely,

Terry Talbert

That was April 1968.

Decades later, long after Terry and her classmates disappeared, six years after I retired, I received an email that astounded me to tears. It deserves to be quoted in full.

January 9, 2013

Dear Dr. Filene,

I am a former student of yours from long ago. I took a 20th Century United States history course you taught in the late 60's while I was an undergraduate history major. I was not a good student, and you would have no reason to remember me. Like many students I regret not being more serious about my studies. I partied my way through the first three years of college and had hardly a serious thought other than ones about myself.

There was a war on at the time and great racial unrest, but I hadn't been impacted directly and couldn't see how I should become involved in any of this. Like too many others, I trusted my government would do the right and necessary things. I stood on the sidelines and made fun of the kids who were standing up for racial equality and against the Viet Nam war.

Most of my academic memories are not particularly good ones. I do, however, have a few positive memories and taking your class was one of these.

Actually your class is one of two I remember best and the one which had the most impact on my thinking and my later life. The strongest memory I have is of your reading aloud from "The Autobiography of Malcolm X." You read a section of the book in which Malcolm describes the elaborate procedures and paraphernalia associated with his people's efforts to straighten their hair. For the first time I really began to understand something of what it must be like to be black in America. Previously I considered myself a tolerant person with fairly liberal views on racial matters, but all of a sudden I came face to face with the fact I hadn't a clue about what the struggles of African-Americans were like or about. I immediately went out and bought a copy of the book and read it cover to cover. I have read it a number of times since.

Somehow the light had come on, and I began to see things I had not previously seen. I came to realize I couldn't put blind trust in anyone or anything. I slowly began to understand what all the campus protests I had formerly ridiculed were all about.

Thirty-five years later I look back on those events and those times and realize what a profound effect they have had on me. It was the time of my awakening, of my growing up, and it all began with the gift of Malcolm X's words spoken by you.

Thank you. If you ever wonder if what you have done with your life had made a difference, I can tell you it has, at least for one person. I will always remember your influence.

Ralph Cooke

Elkin, NC

You're right, Ralph. I remember reading testimonies by Malcolm X and other Blacks, but I don't remember you. More important, until I opened your email, I had no inkling that your inner light had turned on. I feel profoundly moved by your testimony and, once again, I'm amazed by how we teachers perform our work in the dark.

***

Personal Histories

Call me Peter. I was breaching the usual borders of pedagogy. I was throwing classroom windows and doors wide open to the disorderly events of the world at large. I was expressing my interpretations, my personal values, with passion. And some students responded in kind.

Events in 1968 were happening faster than I could keep up with. Half a million American soldiers were fighting in Vietnam. Robert Kennedy decided to run for president, crusading against the war and for social justice. President Johnson announced he would quit at the end of his term. Students at Howard, Columbia, the University of Wisconsin marched, occupied buildings, shut down their campuses in protest against the war and racism. Martin Luther King was murdered. The same day our daughter Becky was born, Robert Kennedy was shot.

How to bear this craziness? I wrote a poem, a kind of blues song, ending with this verse.

> Oh, my baby don't love me yet,
> Sleeping there in her basinette.
> She's only thirty-two minutes old
> And his body's growing cold
> 'round the bullet in his brain.
> We won't see his kind again.
> Oh Bobby, tell us it ain't true,
> What that bullet done to you.

Kennedy's death drove me into disillusioned retreat from the world, but events kept on exploding out there.

In August, a student phoned me from the beach, her voice choked with distress. Had I heard, Russian troops had

A Letter to my Students

invaded Czechoslovakia, what will happen now? Nothing good, I said, stricken that she was calling me, her teacher, who couldn't console her. A week later, I sat in front of our twelve-inch black-and-white TV watching Chicago policemen beat up students protesting outside the Democratic National Convention Hall. Late into the night I sat, weighed down by helplessness.

The pedagogical was inescapably political, but as the fall semester began, I veered toward the personal.

I hoped to find it in Parker Dorm. In the late 1960s, dozens of large public universities across the country sought to improve students' intellectual engagement by creating "residence colleges." Faculty taught courses in dormitories and engaged informally with students on their home turf. Learning and living were brought together as a shared experience. In 1968, UNC followed suit. At the center of campus, across from the football stadium, three adjoining dorms—Avery, Parker and Teague— housing six hundred students were baptized as Scott Residence College. I volunteered to be one of the three Faculty Fellows. I would teach two courses in Parker, hold office hours there, foster stimulating discussions at Wednesday dinners, and mingle with students on weekends. It all was irresistibly promising.

But after an initial flurry of participation at parties and at Wednesday dinners, fewer than a dozen students showed up. During my "office hours" in the lounge, students would stop and chat, but all too often I was disheartened by what they said. What are you planning to take next semester, I asked? Something taught by Professor A or Professor B, they replied, because he's an easy grader. Worse, there was the junior who said he hadn't the slightest idea why he came to college. "What's the point of these history courses?" he said.

"They seem like just a lot of opinions." I explained that reality and truth are complex, and complexity is interesting, but he wasn't listening.

"There are the few who see a light," I wrote in my journal. "But I've given up any idea of converting the campus at large. Conversion converts the convertible."

Unfortunately, I was also feeling defeated in my own realm, the classroom. I had designed a seminar on "American Autobiographies." Benjamin Franklin, Emma Goldman, Gertrude Stein, Malcolm X, and a dozen other characters. How could students resist that fascinating roster! Surely they would fill the room with the chorus of youthful minds exploring the enigma of personal identity across centuries, gender and race. Every week I spent two or three days rereading the books and preparing discussion questions. Every week, a different one of us led a discussion about the autobiographer of their choice. (In my turn, I analyzed Malcolm X's relationship with his father.) And yet, inexplicably, the seminar remained inert. "I had hoped to be only one of 16 instructors," I lamented in my journal, "but it hasn't worked out that way. They depend on me, don't initiate questions, take advantage of freedom (although finally calling me Peter). I assigned short think-pieces, expecting little gems of provocative and imaginative analysis. But instead I got bland, rather trite, and often plain sloppy essays. Similarly, in discussion a few (30%) talk frequently, c. 40% every now and then, 30% never."

I unloaded my frustrations to Bill Coates, one of the gang at those brown-bag teaching lunches. When I was done, he cleared his throat. After twelve years of being told by teachers what to think, he said, students aren't ready to suddenly be autonomous. They need time. More basically, Bill said, I needed to rethink my notion of authority. There's inspiring authority, he said, and suffocating authority. Wasn't I performing a kind of charade in pursuing a collaboration of sixteen equals? They were novices; I was the expert. By acting as if I shrugged off my authority at the classroom door, I inhibited or even demoralized students. The real question was how I could deploy authority in ways that encouraged them to think.

"It has been a hard few months," I wrote in my journal, December 1968, "and I've had to unlearn so many premises. I haven't swerved more than a few students from conventional expectations."

But those few were the saving remnant. Nancy McCharen, Melinda Lawrence, Richie Leonard, Charles Jeffress, Edith Davis, and a dozen others: thank you. During Wednesday office hours we conversed about this and that, anything that was percolating in our minds and lives, and we laughed a lot. Six of us gathered every other Sunday afternoon as a creative-writing club and shared our poems or essays. I was twenty-eight, nine or ten years older, but I considered you "my pals."

***

My breezy first-year honeymoon was over. What now?

I could have retreated to conventional academic territory—back to my classroom in the history department building; back to the library doing research for my second book.

I should have spent more time at home with my family, and devoted more attention to my marriage.

But I didn't.

I joined my pals and together we transported our classroom to the far edge of campus where we tried out a new kind of pedagogy.

The process began on the eve of the spring semester. Nancy, Melinda and Charles were hungry for more structured learning than dinner discussions. They had big questions on their minds, questions about the meanings of freedom and happiness. Could we create a course to find answers, they asked me? Yes, with all my heart, yes. The three Scott College Faculty Fellows—philosopher Maynard Adams, Towny, and I— sat down with them to brainstorm topics and readings—a total of sixty-eight in my frantically scribbled list, which we finally cut to sixteen. "Ideals and Society," we called it—an imposingly boring title to conceal the unruly subject matter from nosy department chairs. Sixty years later, I feel a ripple of excitement as I read the faded-purple mimeographed syllabus of the team-taught seminar.

Week One: I took us headlong into two realms of extreme freedom: the San Francisco psychedelic counterculture of Ken Kesey and his Merry Pranksters, as portrayed in Tom Wolfe's high-octane *The Electric Kool-Aid Acid Test;* and Summerhill in southwest England, A.S. Neill's school without rules. A week later, we swiveled 180 degrees to face Freud's admonitions about *Civilization and Its Discontents.* Three weeks later, under Towny's lead, we explored freedom gone awry or stifled in John Dos Passos's *Big Money* and Ralph Ellison's *Invisible Man.* A thousand pages in two weeks? I can't believe it, but so the syllabus says and, presumably, so the students did. And kept on doing, week after week, until finally Maynard led us through Herbert Marcuse's "Repressive Tolerance" to the existential warning by Dostoevsky's Grand Inquisitor.

A Letter to my Students

Tuesdays and Thursday, 4:30 to 6:00, we met in a basement room of Parker Dorm, three teachers and twenty students tossing big ideas like Frisbees across the table. A few evenings we stayed on to eat dinner and watch a movie: *Lord of the Flies* or *Death of a Salesman*, modern tragedies. A half-century later, I don't remember specifics of lesson plans, essays, grades, just the mood, especially my mood, oh so buoyant in this little underground community of learners.

"Peter—Congratulations!"

One afternoon I found a page of loose-leaf paper taped to my office door, inscribed in loopy pink magic marker.

> Peter—Congratulations!
>
> Couldn't possibly say how completely unanimous your nomination was. Has any <u>other</u> professor been recommended by <u>all</u> his students for a Tanner?
>
> Melinda.

I had received the Lola Spencer and Simpson Tanner Award "in recognition of Excellence in Inspirational Teaching of Undergraduate Students." During the next forty years I would win other teaching awards, but this one was special. It was as if the bell tower had rung my name across the campus. I shivered with pride, and with renewed confidence that, wherever it might take me, teaching was my calling.

***

Teaching is a relationship between pronouns.

The French have two choices: the personal *tu* and the impersonal *vous*. Long ago, English-speakers likewise addressed intimates as *thee*, others as *you*. *Thee* disappeared during the seventeenth century, but some members of the Society of Friends have continued to use it.

I'm not a practicing Quaker, a Friend with a capital F. Still, it's no coincidence that I was educated at Friends Seminary and Swarthmore. No coincidence that I believe everyone harbors an inner light. No coincidence that, whenever possible, I arrange classroom chairs in a circle. All this to set the stage for an engaged and penetrating dialogue with my students: if not *I-Thee*, at least *I-You*.

At the end of "U.S. History since 1933," Betsy Taylor handed me her "Ode to a History Professor."

> For five long years my friends have said
> (art majors, botany, physical ed)
> "Take a course from Peter Filene.
> He's dynamite. You'll see what I mean."
> . . .
> And even though Peter's course meets around lunch
> I guess I could do without food just this wunch.
> And besides, I know all about Disney and hippies
> And Roosevelt, Cold War, and TV, and
> Yipppies.
> I can slide right on through,
> This course is a breeze.
> I can drink, oversleep, come in late as I please.
> So I wandered on in on the third day of class,

A Letter to my Students

Certain that school was a pain in the ass.
And here was this crazy man up at the board
Stalking this way and that—he whispered, he roared!
He cracked a joke, with eyebrows raised
And everyone laughed, but I wasn't fazed.
I'd heard this funny stuff before—
This guy would have to show me more.
Then (hands in his pockets) he said something weird.
I wondered if I could believe what I'd heered.
"What do you people think of this stuff?
I've had my say, but that isn't enough.
We can all seek to learn from each other, you see."
And I just couldn't help it, I had to agree.
. . .
Later I wondered (sipping a beer)
If there wasn't a real change going on here.
A big-time professor who values, he said,
The confusion and chaotic stuff in my head?
This is not what professors are programmed to do.
A new kind of learning just might be emerging
With minds intermingling, conversing, converging.
                   Thank you, Peter
                   (signed) Betsy

P.S. My poetry isn't too hot, but you get the message.
Have a good summer!

I do indeed, gratefully, get your message, Betsy.

In those early years at UNC, though, I wanted more than an *I-You* relationship. I longed for those incandescent occasions when, oh yes, our back-and-forth merged into a heartfelt, symbiotic understanding. An *I-Thee* relationship. That's what I hoped to find at Project Hinton.

***

Project Hinton poster, 1969

"Ideals and Society" came to an end in May, but for Melinda, Nancy and their friends it was just the beginning. They were working with sympathetic faculty and skeptical deans to build a grander version of collaborative education. Not just a course, but a community.

A Letter to my Students

Either you're on the bus or you're off the bus. That was the mantra of Ken Kesey and his Merry Pranksters as they drove across the country tripping on LSD, blaring amplified rock 'n roll, and urging young people in small towns to join the countercultural revolution. At UNC, our curricular bus transported 150 students, three Faculty Fellows (including me) and two resident counselors to the top two floors of a desolate ten-story dorm on the far edge of campus. There we planted Project Hinton, an "Experiment in Coed Living-Learning." Pedagogy turned radically personal.

"It's fun and beautiful, intense but casual, out there. Everyone I talked to has been exhilarated and proud as hell. In fact, this pride of 'us,' 'the experiment,' the 'different' group on campus, is almost tangible."

A month after Project Hinton got underway in the fall of 1969, I wrote a two-page single-spaced letter to Harry Smith, the chaplain who had promoted it before going to Yale.

The 150 students created a non-structured structure for their residence college. Two Wednesdays per month, they gathered for dinner in the nearby cafeteria, followed by a town meeting in a large circle. As you'd expect, I told Harry, the meetings were long, wordy, inefficient, but "infused by a communal spirit, and reaching consensus remarkably easily." A participatory democracy. Instead of entrenched leaders, a new convener, treasurer and so-called senator (ambassador to the dean's office) would be chosen each month randomly among volunteers. In protest against sexism, students sent a male delegate to the campus-wide Association of Women Students. Community news circulated through Whit Bodman's breezy newsletter. Interest groups sprang to life off sign-up sheets in the Lounge: poetry readings; a bridge club; electronic music; you name it.

And there were the unplanned happenings. One cool evening, Nancy sat with Chuck on the top step of the tenth-floor staircase for a guitar lesson. Soon forty or fifty others huddled under blankets on the steps below, singing until midnight. Another evening, dozens of students carpooled to the house of an English professor to read poetry, play instruments, and walk on stilts.

Students had to deal with one very structural impediment, though. The sexes occupied separate floors atop this high-rise dorm, women above and men below, and according to Dean Cansler's edict, they must not commit visitation. After all, even a segregated coed dorm risked outrage from parents, alumni and legislators. During the first month, I told Harry Smith, students behaved virtuously, or at least were misbehaving discreetly. But they were young and this was a participatory democracy. As the semester progressed, they would love each other more freely.

Project Hinton was "fun and beautiful," but what about the learning half of this experiment in living-learning? Towny was teaching a course on American novels. Poet Chuck Wright was talking about aesthetics. And I was teaching a seminar that had emerged the previous spring out of an anguished conversation with two students, Melinda and Richie Leonard. It was a season of violence, not just in Vietnam, not just in black ghettos and outside draft boards and in Berkeley and Madison, but on our own campus. When the black cafeteria workers had gone on strike against unfair treatment, sympathetic students and faculty joined the picket lines and blocked food trucks, some white and black students got into a scuffle, and the governor sent in the National Guard to keep the cafeteria open. How is social justice won or lost? When do the ends justify the means? Melinda and Richie came to me with questions like these? A few hours and several cups of coffee later, we envisioned a seminar on "American Extremism." That fall, I taught it at Project Hinton in tandem with my sociologist friend, Chic Goldsmid.

It turned out to be serious business, and treacherous. Fifteen students, Chic and I confronted the Salem witchhunt, Nat Turner's uprising, the Klan, Anarchism, Black Nationalism, to name some of our weekly topics. And a cascade of questions: What is extremism? Is it abnormal? Is there an extremist personality type? And most disturbing, is extremism necessarily bad? Each week we had more questions than answers as the next case study produced new causes, tactics, ideology and effects. Valiantly we tried and failed to find a pattern of extremism or even, for god's sake, construct a definition. Shortly before Thanksgiving I couldn't escape the terrifying conclusion that we had devoted a semester of our lives to a concept that was meaningless. During forty years of teaching I've experienced countless moments of confusion, but only once a sense of defeat. Experimental pedagogy was more perilous than I'd bargained for.

But Chic, Melinda, Richie and the other students refused to surrender. Through a brain-wrenching discussion, we hammered out a definition that I proudly recorded in the purple ink of "Working Paper #3." *An extremist cannot imagine another viewpoint than his own, because he operates in a closed system, a universe filled with axioms.* Hurrah! With this insight we crowned our seminar with success.

It was a disquieting insight, though. As the Grand Inquisitor declared, some people become extremists to escape ambiguity and uncertainty. At Project Hinton, by contrast, we were into participatory democracy with all its messiness.

"Things have been moving at dynamo rate," I wrote in my journal in late October. I was home only for "brief spurts of time." Two nights a week I ate dinner at Project Hinton, and then on Wednesdays taught my seminar until nine o'clock, after which I would hang around for conversation in students' rooms, sometimes eating cake at someone's birthday party, or meet with the academic innovation committee or sing at a guitar fest, and then go out for a drive with Nancy. Some Wednesdays I was home all of twenty minutes between 8:00 A.M. and midnight.

I confessed some uneasiness. Shouldn't I be trying "to intellectualize the atmosphere," I asked the journal? "But perhaps the whole point," I assured myself, "is for students to see the connections between me-in-the-classroom and me-in-the-nonclassroom world. I would be a model of the blurred line between living and learning."

With Nancy, the line was hard to discern. She was smart, self-confident, alive with curiosity, playful, the object of all her classmates' affection, and of mine. By the time the "Ideals and Society" seminar had ended last spring, she was not only my student; she was my friend. In September, after an evening walk and a kiss, we became ardent friends. We never went further than cuddling as we talked and laughed in the front seat of my car. In the 1980s, the university would outlaw teacher-student dating as inherently exploitative. But Nancy and I believed we were enjoying innocent affection—innocent enough, in fact, that I freely told Jeanette about it. Of course it was more ambiguous than that. Even though I sought equality with students, I possessed more power. Looking back, I see how power inevitably corrupts a relationship. But we live our lives forwards. I was heading into uncharted territory with *I-Thee* as my axiom—on campus and also at home.

A Letter to my Students

Jeanette and I, along with Benjamin (age four) and Becky (age one), had been living in a nondescript two-bedroom rented townhouse. In the fall of 1969, we moved into a four-bedroom house on Gimghoul Drive, a street lined with stately, white-columned structures inhabited by long-established Chapel Hillians. To outward appearance, we had joined the haute bourgeoisie. Truth was, we were living with Hugh and Kathy and their three children ages six to three—they upstairs, we downstairs—in a commune.

Our choice began by chance, although the tumultuous world of the late Sixties rendered it predictable. Jeanette and I had known Kathy (an English grad student) only slightly, and Hugh (an Economics professor) even less, when they dropped in on us the preceding summer. Our conversation centered around my visit to the Providence, Rhode Island, commune of Jeanette's brother Arnie. He and his girl friend and three, sometimes four or five other hippies lived in a tenement apartment amid broken furniture and unwashed dishes. They spent their days on sidewalks selling their underground newspaper, *Extra*, and their nights getting stoned, processing group vibes, and listening to Rolling Stones albums. Hardly the life for us. Still, Jeanette, Kathy and I (to Hugh's annoyance) found ourselves musing about creating our own adult version: "a cooperative household, not a commune," I explained to my journal. We would share the mortgage and daily expenses, kitchen and living room, cooking and baby-sitting, "and most important of all, affection. (Affection is my big word)." But affection within boundaries. "We still reserve privacy, sexual above all, presumably."

As the fall semester began, Kathy said Hugh was on board. On Thanksgiving Day, the two families moved in together. "I should be very changed before June comes around," I prophesied—"not only from Project Hinton, but from Project Gimghoul!"

What followed is a yearlong, tortuous story of joy and grief, passionate ideals and paralyzing confusion. Kathy and I succumbed to flirtation, then to love, and slowly sex insinuated itself into our midst. The four of us cooked lavish meals in the kitchen, danced and kissed in the living room, argued in bedrooms, fled alone on frenzied late-night walks, and increasingly sidestepped questions from friends. The cooperative household evolved into a commune. *I-Thee* melted into a muddled *Us*. A reader leafing through page after late-night, single-spaced typed page of my journal might call it a verbose soap opera. But we were in the middle of it, with no space for irony. We were acting out the unscripted course of Project Gimghoul.

Obviously I've skimmed that story. To fully spell out the details would capsize this essay, which is, after all, about pedagogy. In my day-to-day experience, however, it joined Project Hinton in stirring up my growing bewilderment.

***

I was an award-winning teacher with tenure, but amid the turbulence at home and in the world, I was asking myself *What should I do? Who should I be?* I read Abraham Maslow's *Toward a Psychology of Being* and Rollo May's *Love and Will*. I participated in an encounter group. And I measured myself against the heroics of others.

When Jed Dietz, first my student and soon a dear friend, turned in his draft card, I addressed a poem to him.

A Letter to my Students

> You have become your deed
>
> Which builds higher between us,
>
> Defines me among strangers
>
> Unless I can grow tall enough
>
> To climb to you.

When my student Charles Jeffress decided to leave UNC in his senior year because he objected to the regimen of courses and grades, what he called "education by accumulation," I was again stirred to poetry.

> I lurch into the gear of my thirties,
>
> Heart twitching with the treason.

And in November 1969, I met Jerry Friedberg. I was among eight faculty and students who attended a conference at Michigan State University on experimental colleges. We were giddy as we flew to meet other living-learning pioneers from across the country. The next two days gave us even more than we dreamed of. Out of the panel sessions and the countless conversations over coffee or wine, we returned with bright ideas for making Project Hinton even better.

For me, the meaning of the weekend was Jerry. His background mirrored mine: born in New York City a year before me; Harvard Ph.D. in political science; assistant professor at University of California, Davis. Unlike me, though, he was denied tenure for failing to publish. So now he was teaching at Bensalem College, a subdivision of Fordham. Also unlike me, he was single. At first appearance, Jerry was unremarkable: short, a little paunchy, with a wrinkled shirt. When he spoke, though, he filled the room with a captivating intensity. At the first evening panel, he began with the nuts and bolts of Bensalem's experimental curriculum. But soon his voice grew urgent. Even Bensalem, he said, wronged students with its course requirements and grades. He yearned for a true education, in which learning was organic rather than instrumental. Imagine students and teachers designing courses around questions and problems that really matter to them. For five minutes we sat in total, warm silence. Imagine a community, he said, arms spread wide, where people relate to one another with honesty and feeling.

Another long silence. "I have never been through anything like those beautiful silences," I wrote that night in my journal. I was thrilled. And scared. "He is moving away from college institutions. He is moving toward freedom outside the society."

Yes, Jerry said the next day as we sat and talked one to one, yes, the unknown is a test of courage. We exchanged addresses and hugged goodbye.

>April 3, 1970.
>
>Dear, dear Peter,
>
>>So good to have your letter. I'm just rereading it, touched by your writing a poem for me. Pleased and happy to relive memories of coming to know you a little in East Lansing. I can picture you quite vividly, sitting on the floor with your pipe, slender, thoughtful.
>>
>>I like what you say about your commune. It ties in so much with what's happening in my own life just now. Yes, it's beginning to happen for me, too. I'll enclose 2½ dittoed pages I've just done up so I can tell friends without 40 retellings.

He had left academe, Jerry explained, and traveled across the country visiting communes. Now he found himself with a number of other like-minded people who were planning to lease a place in upstate New York. Seventeen bedrooms, forty acres, and two cows.

> Hell, why don't I come right out with it. You end your letter with words about withering prospects for experimentation at UNC and a sense of waiting, preoccupied with the commune. What leaps to my mind is a fantasy of our coming together for some mutual exploring. I'd love to meet the people you're with, and for all of you to meet the people I'm with. Open-ended. Come to New York City, maybe mid-June.
>
> A warm hello from me to all of yours there.
>
> Love, Jerry

Yes, one would think of course I said *yes* and grasped his hand in quest of freedom or authenticity or whatever it was I was seeking. But I didn't. For longer than a year I would hover between yes and no. Actually, several yeses and nos.

In June our commune broke apart and, with it, our marriages. Now we had four separate Chapel Hill addresses, with children commuting between parents. I lived alone in a trailer at the edge of town, clinging to my children on weekends and to Kathy on occasional weeknights and to the shreds of hope of reuniting with Jeanette.

Meanwhile, I struggled with the contradiction of teaching about freedom and self-actualization from the same lecture notes I had used the year before. "Put up or shut up," I berated myself. "The choice is frightening but clear." In contradiction heaped upon contradiction, I was writing these words in the Library of Congress while doing more research for my book about the history of gender roles.

In the spring of 1971, Jerry came down to Chapel Hill and stayed in Kathy's apartment. He was brimming with stories about the twenty-five fascinating folks in the commune, and the chickens, fresh milk and vegetable garden, and the free love. Come visit us, he said. Give it a try.

I was certainly tempted, although milking cows wasn't my thing, and would I have any time to myself amid all those people, but this was my chance to break free, wasn't it? While I pondered his invitation and earnestly continued teaching, Kathy acted. Off she went to Jerry's commune. Two months later, having graded final exams, I decided to plunge into communal life and, by summer's end, to . . . . To follow Jerry and leave academe? A fearful tremor rose in my chest. Wait and see, I told myself. In any event, Kathy said no, not yet, she needed time on her own. So I went to New Haven.

Why New Haven? Strange, I can't remember what brought me to sublet that two-room apartment above a coffee shop. In any event, there I was, auditioning for various futures. Three days a week I volunteered at a youth crisis center, on the phone with kids tripping on acid or worse, counseling runaways, securing a federal grant for a medical clinic in a Hispanic neighborhood. Nights I read *One Hundred Years of Solitude* and listened endlessly to Carole King. Weekends I visited old friends in Providence, Cambridge, Great Barrington, Old Lyme, enjoying the bittersweet commotion of family life. I considered a job at an institute for radical social change. For a few weeks, I sat in Yale's Sterling Library scribbling notes as I read the diaries and letters of American soldiers fighting in France in 1918—the next chapter in my book. "Be sure I shall play the part well," Alan Seeger wrote his mother, "for I was never in better health nor felt my manhood more keenly." I spent a day and a night with Jeanette, Benjamin and Becky, and came away recognizing our marriage was gone. When can I come see you, I asked Kathy again and again? Not now, she said; no visitors; the commune's having problems. A thirty-year-old Israeli, hitchhiking ten months around the world, showed up at the crisis center looking for a place to crash. *Sometimes I wonder if I'm ever gonna make it home again.*

Days became weeks became August. Time to stop deluding myself. The classroom was my country, and here I was six hundred miles away, in exile. A week before the first day of class I packed my typewriter and books, record albums and clothes, and drove south to Chapel Hill. To my children. And to you, my students. Any twinges of cowardice quickly vanished beneath a surge of relief. I was where I belonged.

* * *

There I stayed until retiring in 2007, thirty-five years, and gradually, my relationship with you, my students, matured. I no longer felt driven to achieve intense, personal connection—*I* with *Thee*—as the proof of success. Meaningful learning, I discovered, would take place while I stayed on my side of the boundary line.

And even if I had tried to be your peer, one learner among many, the passage of time increasingly made that unlikely. "Call me Peter" evolved into being called Dr. Filene. One day a student begged me to let her into my already-full course because "it was my mother's favorite course when she was at UNC." Where once I'd been my students' pal, now I was a stand-in for their parents. Gradually I no longer recognized or could even pronounce the names of the music groups my students listened to. "U.S. History since 1945" stealthily caught up with my life. During my lectures about the Sixties, I mentioned my activity in the Civil Rights Movement and Project Hinton. I had become a piece of historical evidence.

Even more disconcerting, when I threw open the classroom windows and doors to the world at large, an un-Sixties-like wind blew in. For Generation X, Ronald Reagan was an inspiration to compete for material success. *Radical* meant *fanatical* or *crunchy-Granola* if it meant anything at all to these kids. Racism was wrong, but wasn't affirmative action discriminatory? The Vietnam War was a distant mystery. In this new milieu, I struggled to toe the line between teaching passionately and preaching my dogma. Alas, according to some students' anonymous posts on "Rate My Professor," I trespassed.

> (2005) Don't take the class if you are conservative. He is willing to pick on conservatives if you speak up in class.
>
> (2014) One of many who came to his class as conservative, small town kids with half-baked ideas, I left knowing what I believed. Only the most narrow-minded students who didn't like their ideas being challenged found him objectionable. Grade B
>
> (2004) If you love one-sided presentations of history (which if you are at UNC, you probably don't mind) then take this guy. If you are not a bleeding heart liberal, leave him alone. His intolerance for anything to the right of Communism is quite annoying.

A Letter to my Students

> (2006) By far the best history professor Ive ever had. He is very interesting and accessible, and he left discussions open to a WIDE variety of views... people were never attacked for conservative views, even though we all knew he was extremely liberal. TAKE A CLASS FROM HIM, you wont regret it

To bridge the cultural and political gap between me and them, I relied on a two-fold strategy: be enthusiastic about **what** I was teaching, and care about **whom** I was teaching. Most of the time, that pedagogy produced effective learning. And then there were those rare and marvelous occasions when it ignited a student's inner light.

Sometimes the light was a flicker.

"Do you want to hear something weird?" Ashley said as we finished discussing her ideas for her upcoming term paper. "Now I actually look forward to going to the library."

Sometimes the light occurred in improbable fashion.

Two years after taking my "Bohemians, Beats, and Hippies" seminar, Archie wrote me about his work as a law school intern in the N.C. Attorney General's Office. He had to write a case note for the Tennessee Law Review about *Johnson v. California*, 125 S. Ct. 1141 (2005), in which the U.S. Supreme Court called for a strict standard of review when evaluating racial segregation policies in prisons.

> I was ready to deal with the complexities of racial interaction in prison and write the 200 endnotes because, in that seminar, you helped lead me down a daring research trail as we both discovered more about Amiri Baraka. Thanks for the guidance.

At least once, the inner light was too bright to bear.

During a summer school course, a woman in her thirties came to my office worried about the midterm essay. "Listen," I said, "you're making astute comments in class and your writing is superb. My sense is, you don't believe your talent." She was silent, then abruptly got to her feet. "Excuse me, I need the restroom." A few minutes later she was back, her face flushed from having wept. "No one every told me that before," she said.

And I'm forever grateful to students like Elizabeth Manekin, who shone and shone and shone.

> I think it's impossible to know what direction I might've taken if I hadn't met and worked with you, Peter. My thesis would've been much less fun. Had you not squelched my hopes of become an academic (smile) and pointed me toward work with the public, I might've never found my present path. So I thank you for helping me make sense of things—from my jumbly thought processes to the way that I am. And I thank you for being a true mentor and friend throughout the journey.

Thank you, Elizabeth, and the thousands of other students who have enlivened me all these years.

With warmest wishes,

Peter

Chapter 8

The Cure for Love

A year after Jeanette and I officially divorced in 1972, I fell in love with Kathy.

She was twenty to my thirty-three, a student in my classroom, a would-be writer—make that a beautiful, silky-haired, Carolina writer with Matisse-blue eyes and a habit of silence—in sum, the woman of mystery I always dreamed and never believed I might . . . what is the correct verb? . . . *acquire? possess?* Well, let's settle for *have*. So when she allowed me a burst of laughter through her silence, and later, after she graduated, a kiss, and much later her nakedness, I thought I had her. Once you have found her, never let her go.

We strode into McDonald's as Romanian refugees, ordering French fries with extravagant gestures and throaty accents. She posed for my camera on the living room couch under a hot photo lamp—Georgia O'Keeffe to my Alfred Stieglitz—her bare breasts gathering creamy light. I played harmonica to her guitar, Dylan to Joni Mitchell, "Oh I could drink a case of you, darling, and I would still be on my feet." We co-starred in our private movie with a sound track of our own making. I celebrated her in a poem.

> I woo you not
> to wedding or wife,
> but always the ambush of your humors
> like salt wind in my mouth.
> I would make music with you
> and a house around us
> and love with you
> and hopes for us.

We moved into a little house by a highway at the edge of town and, a couple of years later, rented a bigger house all by our lonesome at the end of a dirt driveway on a former tobacco farm ten miles outside Chapel Hill. While she commuted west to the UNC-Greensboro creative writing program, I commuted east to UNC. She critiqued my photographs and I critiqued her stories. We acquired Shiloh from the county shelter, a klutzy black Lab who liked to run away and whom I would retrieve from a neighbor's porch.

So how did this go wrong?

After she left me, I came up with all sorts of wrong answers—rageful, self-pitying, teary, a little crazed. Now, in the cool of four decades gone, I'm ready to hear her side of the story.

I drag the dusty cardboard box from the closet and, oh my god, I can't believe all these letters she wrote me, hundreds of letters dated Wednesday, Saturday, nothing more, but here they await me in chronological order in their manila folders because, from our first days together, I assumed we would be memorable.

I should have recognized a warning in this plenitude. We were gone from each other as much as we were together.

She was writing from the Vineyard (waitressing) and Albuquerque (dog-grooming course) and Chapel Hill (secretarying); writing to me in Chapel Hill (where I was teaching, and caring for my children) and Cambridge (researching) and Maine and Providence (in photography workshops).

> Sweetheart, how I miss you when I realize you aren't here.

Strange, at first I don't recognize her handwriting.

> So many times I keep thinking that you will pop up from around the corner, harmonica in hand, demand Chelsea Morning be sung or such. You are incredibly here.

Wherever "here" was, for me it was somewhere else.

> I'm not in love with you conveniently—I am in love with you totally, and all areas of me are involved. And for the first time in my life I want that totality. And there is no panic about consumption. I feel too confident about my warning signals and your perceptions to feel threatened that I will lose myself into you.

But what kind of love thrives on words on paper?

Our separations proved we were free to leave and yet

belonged together, a daring *pas de deux*, or so we bragged.

> And what am I obliged to do now with Peter, with the man who loves me a little like Harold [Nicolson] loved [his wife] Vita [Sackville-West, who had a love affair with a woman], letting me leave to come back on my terms and love him but we have written so much of this we have talked it forever and Chapel Hill still another test, it will go on forever if we last, forever because he will not grasp me like Harold wouldn't and tell me to quit fucking up what we have, and me always running one little step further because I have been cooped up for so long . . . Peter, Peter who I love very much, love me enough however much that turns out to be I am not mad, only unsettled.

Rivers of words typed on cheap paper gone yellow or scribbled on lined stationery, page after page,

> COME HOME! so I can wrap my superpowerful thighs around you and hold you in a "clinch" for a while to re-realize you

Addressed to Dear Babes, Sweetheart, Lover, names that chime in my ear like distant off-pitch bells. Did we ever call each other by name?

As I turn the pages like calendar leaves, 1976, 1977, her voice grows stronger, surer

> Sorry about last night's phone call. I was feeling too depressed to take much advice, and I know you were trying hard, we just seemed to be going in opposite directions. Also when I heard you

> sounding so formal and distant it didn't help, most of the time I was sort of half crying anyway and not wanting to get into a full boo-hoo so you would be left stranded, trying to cope with that.... Anyway, it was a crummy way to use up money.

Her voice grows hard-edged, knowing, critical. She sees me all too clearly, too coolly. I'm feeling the same flutter of fear I felt back then.

> My good friends know my bitchy, practical, intellectual, crafty, obsessive—all sides. They know the madman and the saint. You are saint, my love, to too many people. Good old Peter. What would your best friend Walker do if you zoomed into his office one day and had a screaming fit? Probably love you for it. Am I sounding preachy? Don't mean to, hon. But I know the child, the man, everything, and I want you to be able to be all.

The past is rushing in on me.

I thought I had her, but she wouldn't be had.

Only a handful of letters remain at the bottom of the cardboard box. I want to shout a warning about trouble ahead.

***

I'm in a phone booth at O'Hare Airport explaining my flight is delayed an hour, ice on the runway, I hope to be home by dinner time, but good news, they loved my presentation at the conference ... when Kathy interrupts me: "Do you want to get married?"

"What?" I say.

"Married." She laughs.

I can't breathe. I try to catch the eye of people rushing past the glass door from somewhere to somewhere else with suitcases and children, as if one of them can counsel me, but I'm alone with the voice of the woman I love desperately.

"Babes?" she says. "You still there?"

"Yes," I shout, and a circle of mist blooms on the glass. So it's going to turn out happily after all. "Yes, I'd love to get married."

Four months later, we marry in her brother's back yard. Three years later, I'm sitting on the edge of our bed in North Carolina and she's in a phone booth outside the Provincetown Writers' Workshop. "I'm sorry," she says for the third time.

"How could you, Kathy!"

"At least I'm being honest."

"About falling in love with that artist? A shitty kind of honesty."

I've had a long time to reflect upon all this, half my life by now, and I still don't understand. I don't mean her adultery. We were hanging on by a thread as thin as a telephone wire, so sooner or later something—an argument, an affair, or simply fatigue—was going to do the damage. No, what I don't understand is why Kathy proposed marriage. She knew better. As she wrote years later: "When I finally married, I avoided a church setting, my skittishness and claustrophobia too well ingrained by then. I knew I couldn't finish a walk down any aisle." But her resistance lay deeper than church.

"I felt disoriented and weirdly allergic. Less than three hours into forever, I'd broken out in hives."[1]

But I'm dodging the real question. Standing in that airport phone booth, why did I say yes? I could have said, "not before we see a marriage counselor, talk about our trips and my kids and the cooling of sex and the thirteen years' gap between us." But that's not exactly a romantic response. In fact, it's a longwinded way of saying no. I said yes, because—as I understood even then, in that phone booth—I was grabbing the contrary-to-all-the-evidence hope of salvaging the grand love we began with.

***

If only I'd learned about having and holding before I met her. I had tenure. I had two young children whom I desperately loved. On weekends I tried to make us a family of four but Kathy stayed away at dinnertime and sidestepped their hugs, unready to be a twenty-five-year-old stepmother, and who can blame her, but I did. I hugged the children of my broken marriage. I clutched my lover, like a man drowning. The trouble was, she needed to save herself.

Here's her last letter, spring of 1980. At the time I almost tore it into shreds, but settled for bursting into tears. Now I read it with respect. Outside of my awareness—or let's be honest: against my wishes—my former student had finally completely graduated.

> I guess I'm trying, will try to tell you what I have found clearly about myself, about us since coming back [to Provincetown] from NC. We are no help to each other. We have tried

to be, you even more than me, I think, but your helping was so many times a hindrance. By loving me as you did, you helped me keep me down. Please understand that I know the motive was love (not in any way malicious) but unfortunately the effect is the same. There is such a basic wrong between us that, from my perspective, we can't stay in any kind of married state.

To have and to hold. As you would guess, I had trouble letting go.

It was a Saturday morning when she phoned from the Provincetown Artists Workshop and said she had fallen in love with a painter. I sat on the bed for an hour afterwards watching the wasps bang against the window.

***

After she left me, I was afraid of the night. Arguments chased her inside my dreams like crazy music until I lurched awake thinking the phone had rung. The dark side of the moon of love. I slept an hour, maybe five if I was lucky. It's amazing what you can do—teach students, chat with colleagues, pay bills—with your mind screeching like a smoke alarm. I stood in the classroom and told my students about the Great Depression, FDR, New Deal, although my voice seemed to belong to someone else.

During my first divorce I thought I'd learned how to grieve, but I was wrong. Anguish comes in many guises.

Sobs spilled out of me at a red light or in the middle of a Joni Mitchell song or finding her socks under the bed. I

The Cure for Love

wondered why people in the grocery store didn't notice my wounds. I lost hunger, except for sweets. My pants dangled on my hips.

Our dog Shiloh, now my dog, ran away and I marched to my neighbor's porch and dragged him home. In the dead of night, I sat at the kitchen table drinking red wine and writing poems saturated in bitter self-pity while Shiloh slept at my feet. I played harmonica along with *Blood on the Tracks*, standing alone in the living room, and believe me, I respected her for doin' what she did and gettin' free, but oh man, the bitter taste lingered on from the nights I tried to make her stay.

I shot pictures of children climbing on a jungle gym, riding fathers' shoulders, strangers' children. On weekends with my son and daughter, I smiled, but they sensed my sorrow and pressed their tender bodies closer.

I talked with a therapist and forgot what he told me. I preferred to run. I ran down the country road as far as the hill. The next day I ran up the hill. I began running two miles, three, five, as if I could outrun my misery. Rain or shine, I ran, waging arguments with Kathy with each punishing throb of my legs. "I'm not your student any more," she shouted. "I loved you," I shouted back.

Eventually I found the cure for love.

It was in my darkroom, that narrow rectangle hollowed out of the world beside our house—my house now. Four feet wide, eight feet long. A counter and a sink, a square clock, a stool. A row of bottles holding developer, stop bath, fixer, toner. I set the silver developing tank and roll of film on the counter. Switched off the light. Stretched my arms wide, touching wall and wall, and let daily things fall away from me. Midterm exams, telephone calls, Provincetown, all gone. In here the clock's pale green hands measured private time, sweeping backwards to zero. In here I was alone but not lonely.

Children bathe in D-76 developer inside the tank for six-and-a-half minutes at sixty-eight degrees, then stop bath and a twenty-minute rinse, emerging under the amber safelight as miniature, glossy negatives. I select one to enlarge eight-by-ten inches on low-contrast No. 2 Ilford paper, fifteen seconds, no, next time try No. 4 at twenty-two seconds, scrutinizing every feature, every shadow, rendering the children beautiful. Then the magical moment: slide the print into the developer bath and watch the positive image gradually materialize, line by line, tone by tone, out of the shimmery silver nitrate. Rock the tray, rubbing two fingers across the cheek to make it darker. Look! I've made something beautiful out of nothing.

And if I've committed a mistake, misjudged something along the way, I can start all over again and do it right.

1   Kat Meads, "Exchanging Forever," The Missouri Review, reprinted in Born Southern and Restless (Pittsburgh: Duquesne University Press, 1996) 124-25.

Chapter 9

THE ART OF LOST AND FOUND

On a balmy May afternoon in Paris in 2015, I lost my sense of direction. I was standing at the corner of rue du Temple and rue des Francs-Bourgeois with a map in my hand, trying to make my way back to my hotel after a day of shooting photographs. I was here, where my finger indented the page, and the hotel at Arts et Métiers was there, a few inches up and to the left—northwest— but when I headed left on rue des Francs-Bourgeois, the setting sun was behind me, which meant I was heading east. So I turned around and studied the map, but east and west kept changing places. I became frightened now. Seventy-five years old, alone, without a smartphone. It was like one of my dreams of getting lost in a maze of alleys and faceless buildings, but I was desperately awake.

I turned around again, toward the sun, a little dizzy. I closed my eyes and sent myself back to my childhood in Manhattan, facing uptown with the East River on my right, the Hudson on my left. But when I looked down again at my finger on the map, the streets skittered. Was I having a stroke? Was I going to collapse on the sidewalk, here, three thousand miles from my children and friends?

If only I had a smartphone, but back then I prided myself on doing fine without that gadget. Better to keep my mind clear and both hands free while I shot photographs.

Pedestrians hurried past me. The traffic light went from green to red to green. I stuffed my Nikon and the map into my backpack and headed blindly across the street into the Parisian mêlée. Eventually, by trial and error I arrived at my hotel.

I felt betrayed. By maps, for one thing. Contrary to previous moments when I got lost, a map had failed to rescue me. The correspondence between flat cartography and all-around-me reality had ruptured. I also felt betrayed by aging. My internal GPS, which I had always relied on, had abruptly lapsed. But shadows come with sunlight. In the wake of this distressing incident, I would make a breakthrough as a fine art photographer.

***

The first time I saw Paris wasn't the first time. Or so I heard myself saying to Jeanette in our rented VW as we drove from Brussels through the *banlieues*. "I feel as if I've been here before," I said. It was 1963, the start of a month-long vacation from the thousand index cards for my dissertation. "I know, Jen, that doesn't make sense, but . . . ." I didn't believe in former lives, and yet, could it have been just from reading Hemingway and Camus that I felt at home? A *frisson* rippled on my neck, the signal of something wilder than reason. I steered through the hurlyburly of Parisian traffic, fearlessly, no need for a map, and arrived at our hotel on rue Jacob. As we started to unpack in our tiny fourth-floor room, I tugged Jeanette onto the bed and, with the voices of pedestrians floating up through the window, we made love with special urgency. "Oh my god," she murmured afterwards, "I forgot the diaphragm." I should have been worried, but I found myself smiling at our recklessness.

I've gone to Paris numerous times since that first visit— with Jeanette and then Kathy and then Erica, my former wives— but as I became intrigued with shooting artistic photographs, more often than not I went alone.

Flâneur: from the Old Norse verb *flana*, "to wander with no purpose." The *flâneur* emerged in Paris in the mid-nineteenth century. He is "the painter of modern life," Charles Baudelaire exclaimed. "His joy is to be away from home and yet to feel at home anywhere." Or as Victor Fournel wrote in 1867, the art of *flânerie* is *"un daguerréotype mobile et passioné* (a moving, passionate photograph) of the movement of the city and the public spirit."

I wandered the streets and museums with camera in hand, waiting for the exquisite scene or the dramatic moment. It was a meditative practice. A serene alertness. I entrusted myself to Paris and one afternoon in 1994 I had a moment, a violently happy moment, of discovery.

I had just shot a photo of those elegant gray Parisian shutters and grimaced in frustration, remembering how all my previous photos of shutters had fallen short of the beauty in front of me. If only I could paint on the photograph, but I was no painter. Then I noticed the abstract landscape in a gallery window, a graceful patchwork of greens and oranges. Why not! I pushed the little lever on my Nikon FM to click the shutter without advancing the film, and shot the painting. When I returned to Chapel Hill, developed the prints, and saw the double exposure, I rejoiced. A painterly photograph!

Shoot an image of a person or scene. Then push the lever to cock the shutter again and look for a work of art that may be the perfect mate when superimposed upon the image waiting on the film and inside my head. Click a second time. Walk on. I won't know the results until the film is developed. If I'm lucky, one or two out of thirty-six will be a *daguerréotype mobile et passioné*. The ghostly members of Renoir's boating party mingle among a group of tourists in the Musée d'Orsay. A young woman smoking a cigarette in the Tuileries Garden is clothed in the marble of the statue beside her. Double exposures are born in a marriage between intention and chance. Like traveling without a map.

Paris Façade, double exposure, 1994

Smoking in the Tuileries, double exposure, 2003

Learning to read words is a kind of magic trick. I watched with awe as each of my grandchildren one day, presto, transformed the black squiggles on a page into sounds that represented things, events and concepts. Reading a map is an even more difficult magic. It entails place-finding and way-finding. Preschoolers can use a treasure map to find an object in the room. But using a map to navigate from here to there is beyond their capacities. Only by the age of nine or ten can children perform the leap from two dimensions to three.

London taxi drivers have to learn 320 routes along some 25,000 streets before they can earn their license. When a cognitive neuroscientist studied the cabbies' brains, she found their right posterior hippocampus was significantly larger than in the general population. That's the region containing so-called place cells. They fire off electrical impulses whenever we enter a familiar location, with each bundle of active cells corresponding to a particular place. It's a neural representation of an internal cognitive map.

But recognizing a route or place isn't the same as having a sense of direction, a sense of one's place in relationship to the whole. That function is located beside the hippocampus in the entorhinal cortex. Scientists have recently found evidence of so-called grid cells that fire in a repetitive pattern anchoring our bodies in the surrounding environment. In other words, they function as an internal GPS system.

Alas, as we age, our grid cells may fire weakly or in spasms. Although I could read the map in my hand at the corner of rue du Temple and rue des Francs-Bourgeois, I didn't know which way to walk. For other disabilities, we employ familiar remedies: hearing aids; cataract surgery; walkers and wheelchairs. For a faltering sense of direction, we can rely on a magical device operating in tandem with manmade planets: the global navigation satellite system launched in the 1980s by the Department of Defense and made available in the 1990s to civilians. Maps have become obsolete. Our smartphone not only shows us where we are; with an imperturbably patient voice, it guides us mile by mile, turn by turn, along the journey to our destination.

Paradoxically, though, the remedy also magnifies the disability it's intended to solve. A 2010 study found that older adults who reported regularly using GPS to navigate had less activity and less grey matter in their hippocampus compared to those who didn't. They also performed slightly worse on a cognition test. By turning on the smartphone, they forfeit some brain power. Still, it's a sensible tradeoff. Old folks don't roller skate, after all. They watch their step. They journey in a Road Scholar van with a guide along a predefined itinerary.

I used to pity those tourists. Faithful to the art of *flâneurie*, I wandered heedlessly, happily, losing myself. But at the corner of rue du Temple and rue des Francs-Bourgeois, age caught up with me, and like it or not, I had to reckon with the consequences. Two years later, I decided, grudgingly, I'd do better relying on a Road Scholar tour than on my map-reading to take me through Portugal and, I have to admit, it was a relief. No deciphering of train schedules and maps. Sit back and be delivered to walled villages, vineyards and cathedrals. With equal grudgingness, I acquired a GPS for driving to destinations where I used to navigate by the seat of my pants, or entorhinal cortex. Better that annoying know-it-all voice than a flustered late arrival at the concert. "Hey, Peter," I murmured on the verge of my eightieth birthday, "you're not seventy-two anymore."

And then there's my art work. While all my fellow photographers have gone digital, I've clung to film. The digital camera cannot make double exposures. It shoots an image, displays it, and moves on automatically for the next shot and the next and the next, a voracious consumption of the world. Intention and chance become divorced. By contrast, when I shoot on film I take time between making one image and the second, and I can't know until later whether I succeeded. I engage in what Rebecca Solnit calls "a voluptuous surrender" to not foreseeing. It's "an art," she writes:

> of keeping your balance amid surprises, of collaborating with chance, of recognizing that there are some essential mysteries in the world

and thereby a limit to calculation, to plan, to control. To calculate on the unforeseen is perhaps exactly the paradoxical operation that life most requires of us.

"Yes," I echo. But here's another paradox. After twenty-five years of shooting double exposures, I have to confess the practice began to feel safe. I found myself trying to repeat previous images rather than risking something new. If I was going to keep creativity alive, I had to renew the chance of getting lost. But not at the corner of rue du Temple and rue des Francs-Bourgeois.

Blues If You Want, photocollage, 2019

I sat at the kitchen table and began tearing apart old photographs and combining the pieces into new images. The boy who stood in a Washington, D.C. museum now looks over a fence in Dublin. A woman walks through blue strips of a De Kooning canvas. Image-making without traveling.

Through the process of photocollage, I travel in unexpected directions while sitting at home.

Finally, more generally, and most important of all, I arrive at the question of how to navigate through the remainder of my life. One pays a price to be a *flâneur*, after all. Bipedal walking is unique to humans, and it enables us to have hands free and use tools (like a camera) and to see into the distance. Yet it's remarkably unsteady. Perilous. Unlike four-footed creatures, at any moment we can fall with dire consequences. Given this vulnerability, anthropologists speculate, bipedal walking prompted our species to form tribes and to put our trust in others.

This week I bought tickets to visit Paris next spring. Paris again, but with a difference. Although I'll take my Nikon and a map, I'll also travel with the woman I love. I picture us walking slowly, hand in hand, wary of cobblestones, mindful of her arthritic knee and my sore quadriceps. Can there be a pair of *flâneurs*? Not according to Baudelaire. Well then, I'll forsake the art of *flâneurie*. Indeed—another confession—in those evenings after joyfully wandering all day alone with my camera, I often felt lonely.

Next spring I want to share Paris with my love in a voluptuous surrender.

Postscript, June 2021: Talk about a divorce between intention and chance! Six months after I wrote this essay, the pandemic forced everyone to huddle at home. Paris closed and I canceled our tickets. *Quel dommage!*

Lynn S. Liben, "The Road to Understanding Maps," *Current Directions in Psychological Science*, 18, no. 6 (Dec. 2009), 310-15.
Garfield, 411-112; Simon Makin, "The Brain Cells behind a Sense of Direction," *Scientific American*, June 2015); https://www.medicaldaily.com/sense-direction-where-am-i-get-lost-378977; Eleanor A. Maguire, David G. Gadian, et al., "Navigation-related Structural Change in the Hippocampi of Taxi Drivers," Proceedings of the National Academy of Sciences, USA, 97, (April 11, 2000), 4398–4403. doi:10.1073/pnas.070039597; Elisabeth Hollister Sandberg and Janellen Huttenlocher, *Journal of Cognition & Development*, Vol. 2 Issue 1 (Feb. 2001), 51-70.
Antonia Malchik, "Walkability is at the Heart of Human Societies," -https://historynewsnetwork.org/article/172786
Rebecca Solnit, "Open House," A Field Guide to Getting Lost (New York: Penguin Books, 2005), 5-6.

Chapter 10

Quarantining with Heidegger

The spring of 2020 brings the promise of death, especially to the already old. The coronavirus is racing from China to Europe to New York City, devouring hundreds of thousands and leaving countless others breathing to the merciless rhythm of machines.

Public health authorities direct us to "shelter in place."

I'm a step ahead, I think. On March 18, I happily moved to the Carol Woods retirement community in Chapel Hill, to a one-bedroom cottage brimming with sunlight. I felt like a freshman entering college again, awaiting new friends, Wednesday concerts, Thursday lectures, who knows. But shelter has turned into a cell. Instead of the cheerful din of the dining-room, meals arrive in cardboard containers with a knock on my cottage door. Before the pandemic, I delivered Meals on Wheels every Tuesday morning to eight or ten clients who greeted me in pajamas or a wheelchair or in bed with a smile, a joke, "can't complain," "God bless," while the TV flickered in their shaded rooms. With the ninety-six-year-old novelist Daphne Athas who wouldn't wear her hearing aids, I held shouted conversations about the evils of Trump and the etymology of *demagogue*, her delight rereading *War and Peace*, or memories of her Greek immigrant father, while I placed the plastic dinner tray in her fridge and laid today's banana beside yesterday's brown banana. In February, alas, Daphne fell and was taken to rehab, where she has been denied visitors.

As am I. Shelter in place has become quarantine, derived from *quaranta giornia*, forty days during which all ships arriving in Venice during the fifteenth-century plague were required to sit at anchor before passengers and crew could go ashore. Forty days and nights. Nine hundred and sixty hours. The long cottage silences are punctuated by shrill newscasters and the wavery voices of friends on cell phone and Zoom. And visits by Stuart, my beloved lady.

On our first date six years ago, I heard myself saying, totally out of the blue, "if we're going to have any kind of relationship, Stuart, I need to know whether you like romantic comedies." "I do," she said. We've been living alone together ever since, laughing at our foibles. Before the pandemic, she joined me for evenings in my Carrboro apartment. Amid the quarantine, she furtively arrives in my cottage like a student sneaking in a dorm, although a six-foot-tall, blond, beautiful woman with a wide white hat can hardly count on furtivity. She arrives at my door with romaine lettuce, cherry tomatoes, a ripe avocado, green onions and a lemon, out of which she constructs an elaborate salad to accompany the Carol Woods chef's variant of pasta and veggies that I sauté and spice back to life. Stuart takes food seriously. And friendships. Her incandescent smile warms everyone in her radius. Especially me.

Quarantining with Heidegger

By April, hospitals in New York City have become as crowded as rush-hour subways, with patients lying in hallways gasping for life. Then similar scenes appear in Los Angeles, Atlanta, the Midwest. Three-fourths of Americans are under lockdown. How much longer? We'll enjoy normal life by Easter, Trump proclaims. Just wait and see.

In my cottage, quarantine gives rise to urgent existential questions that I long ago settled or shelved in a dusty corner of my brain. What is the point of surviving however long—months; years—imagining how my body and mind will deteriorate into nothingness? And how shall I get through the next two hours until dinner? I made a career teaching United States history, but I won't find answers there. "Life becomes ideas," the French philosopher Merleau-Ponty wrote, "and the ideas return to life." I'm desperate to breathe the air of lofty ideas.

***

One afternoon I come upon Wolfram Eilenberger's *Time of the Magicians: Wittgenstein, Benjamin, Cassirer, Heidegger, and the Decade that Reinvented Philosophy*. Of the four philosophers, whom I've heard of but never read, Heidegger seems the loftiest and maybe most helpful. There he is, alone in his hut a century ago, hammering out *Sein und Zeit* (*Being and Time*). Time I had all too much of, and not enough being to fill it with.

I knock on the door of his wood-shingled hut overlooking a green valley high up in the Black Forest. The man who greets me looks more like a peasant than a philosopher in his brown farmer's jacket and knee-length breeches. He is small, lean, with tiny black eyes and a bow-shaped mustache above a pinched mouth. Not much to look at. But as his students at the University of Marburg can testify, Professor Heidegger is charismatic. When he enters the classroom, he carries an air of danger, ready to send the edifice of traditional philosophers crashing down upon their heads. "Thinking has come to life again" in his lectures, according to one student, Hannah Arendt. "Thinking as . . . a passion. Thinking and aliveness become one." Heidegger dares to plunge into the momentous question unanswered since the Greeks fifteen hundred years ago: *What is the meaning of "Being"?*

Being is around us, he says. We have a preconceptual understanding of it—an everyday understanding. If I say "There is a chair," you ask no questions.

But think about that little verb *is*, Heidegger says. What does it mean to say anything *is*? There is a chair and there is a cat, but where is Being with an uppercase B? *Sein.* Isness. Chairs and cats don't worry about this question. Only humans do, so the answering takes off from you and me.

There's a knock on my door and I drop the book, grateful to be called away from Heidegger's boggling question. Inside the cardboard container I find goat cheese macaroni with steamed spinach and baked butternut squash. Soon Stuart arrives with a kiss, salad makings, and another episode of the mouse. Three nights she has put peanut butter in the Have-a-Heart trap and each morning no peanut butter, no mouse. "A Political Science professor," she laments, "is outwitted by a mouse!"

"You've created a cushy welfare program," I say.

"I consoled myself with a breakfast of poached egg with two asparagi, plus a slice of perfectly ripe avocado on toast."

Oh Stuart, my beloved queen of the quotidian.

"And how are you getting along with Heidegger?" she says.

"Not well. He reminded me of a long-ago afternoon when I was a history graduate student drinking coffee in Hannah Arendt's New York apartment. I'd finagled the invitation through my mother, who'd been a friend of Hannah's in Weimar Germany."

"Wow. Lucky you."

I shake my head. "All I remember is Arendt abruptly asking a question in German and me like an idiot, tongue-tied."

"Failed the pop quiz, eh?" Stuart says, and we laugh together.

***

In the morning I resume where I had left that strangely intoxicating verbal music high in the Black Forest. "What is the meaning of: '*es gibt*' (there is)," Heidegger demands? "Again: the question is not whether *es gibt* chairs or tables, or houses or trees, or sonatas by Mozart or religious powers, but whether *es gibt* means anything whatsoever." He pauses for a beat. "And what does anything whatsoever mean? Something universal—indeed, one might say, the most universal, that applies to every possible object."

Heidegger is twenty-nine, delivering his very first lecture at the University of Freiburg, when he speaks those words. Three years later, in 1922, he spends eight days talking philosophy with his friend Karl Jaspers. Jaspers, a young psychologist and philosopher, has made a splash with his book about how people experience a sense of authenticity in the face of death. Germans are all too familiar with death. After four years of the Great War, one of every five German men is dead or maimed or suffering shell shock. Peace has brought hunger and angst along with political unrest: Communists versus monarchists versus Nazis versus republicans. Worse, many Germans chew on a bitter fantasy about why they were defeated. The Kaiser's omnipotent army, they believe, was stabbed in the back by Jews.

"I enjoyed our eight days of 'symphilosophising,'" Heidegger exclaims to Jaspers. "A friendship came toward us, the growing certainty of engaging in a common struggle, sure of itself on both 'sides'—all of that remains uncannily in my mind, just as the world and life are uncanny for the philosopher."

But now he needs to be alone in his hut in the Black Forest. "When I have been meeting new people," he explains to his wife, who has stayed home with their two sons in Marburg, "I notice I am essentially indifferent to them all—they walk past outside as if on the other side of the window.... The great calling to a transtemporal task must always also be a condemnation to solitude."

That task is to decipher the ontological mystery of Being (*Sein*). It is a lonely task. Each of us, as an individual *Dasein* ("being there"), must undertake the work on his own. "Factual *Dasein*, whatever it is, is only ever the fully own, not the just-being of general humanity. In each case mine (*Jemeiniges*)."

***

This sounds like nonsense, I tell myself, as I close the book and walk to the kitchen. But give it time and an open mind, like when I first stepped into James Joyce's *Ulysses*.

"A dollop of brie cheese did the trick," Stuart jubilantly announces at dinner. "This morning I found the mouse in the trap and took him—or her? or they, as we're supposed to say these days—to run free in the woods."

I'm about to take salad out of the bowl when she says, "Wait! Before you mess it up, look how beautiful it is."

I gaze at the undulant, gleaming landscape encircled by ceramic blue, and it is beautiful. "Thank you," I murmur.

Heidegger is waiting for me in the morning. *Dasein* won't find true knowledge of Being by taking courses in sociology or psychology, he explains. Search not in the ivory tower but in the everyday world. "This is the way in which everyday Dasein always *is*: when I open the door, for instance, I use the latch." The path toward answers involves what Heidegger calls "projects." Cut wood for the stove. Hammer nails to fix a floorboard. "The less we just stare at the hammer-Thing , and the more we seize hold of it and use it, the more primordial does our relationship to it become." *Handlichkeit*. While you are employing the hammer, it acquires for you a "readiness-to-hand," your particular Being.

I find myself growing busy with projects. Or as the philosopher and novelist Iris Murdoch put it, I "inhabit" myself with projects. I make a loaf of herb and onion bread, enjoying the steady rhythm of kneading the dough with flour-dusted hands. Maybe this is how authenticity feels. Unable to take my camera to New York or Paris where I shot the photographs that hang in FRANK Gallery and on my cottage walls in Chapel Hill, I improvise. I tear old prints into strips and combine them into collages. *Voila!* The familiar double-exposures are reborn into multilayered images that intrigue me all over again.

I lay out three of them on the coffee table. Stuart picks them up tenderly at the edges one at a time. "I'm not sure, is this supposed to be a child?" "Oh, I love this one." "Sorry, this black blob is just. . . " and she makes a face. Silently I protest against that "not-sure" and "blob," but a few days later I recognize she's right as usual.

**

Forty days have stretched to sixty, eighty, one hundred and twenty, interminable. New cases of Covid in the U.S. hit a record daily high. Thousands of people lie in hospital beds gasping for breath. One hundred thousand Americans are dead, more than during the Korean and Vietnam wars combined. The virus rampages like invisible wolves. No, like swarms of bees. When I was stung forty years ago, I spiraled helplessly down toward the darkness of extinction en route to the emergency room and the miracle of epinephrine. No, neither wolves nor bees—people, friends and strangers, everyone is a possible killer with one cough of a microscopic droplet. Thursdays, senior discount day at the grocery store, I dash masked through the aisles grabbing bread, broccoli, yogurt and bananas and return to my cottage breathless and sweaty.

One morning I wake up with pain throbbing on the right side of my jaw. The next morning it's worse. Root canal? Cancer? I make an emergency appointment with my dentist. He and the hygienist, outfitted like astronauts, probe and X-ray. "Just a bruise," he says, finally. "From clenching your jaw. This month we've had an unusual number of patients clenching, grinding, even cracking teeth."

In July, Stuart undertakes a project more daunting than salad. Her name has risen to the top of the Carol Woods waiting list, and a cottage has become available just down the path from mine. Now she has to outfit it. Week after week she struggles with countless quandaries about cabinet doors (maple or oak? light or dark?), counter tops (quartz or granite?), towel bars (round or square?), and so on and so forth. She is making that cottage *jemeineges*, fully her own. Soon we'll be even closer to each other.

***

I'm deep into reading *At the Existential Café* by Sarah Bakewell when the phone rings. It's Daphne Athas's nephew in California, who's sorry to tell me she died two weeks earlier, alone. There will be some kind of memorial ceremony after the pandemic. I picture Daphne struggling to finish *War and Peace* in time. That evening I weep in the shelter of Stuart's arms.

May. In Minneapolis, a white policeman handcuffs George Floyd, throws the black man to the sidewalk and presses his left knee on Floyd's neck for nine minutes. "I can't breathe," Floyd gasps. *Black Lives Matter!* Huge crowds protest peacefully from New York's Times Square to Hanalei Pier in Hawaii. There are also, as always, small groups who loot and commit arson. President Trump urges police to maintain law and order, shooting protestors if need be. In the early 1960s I marched and picketed and sang "We Shall Overcome" in the streets of Boston. Amid the pandemic, I join a dozen white-haired residents at the front gate of Carol Woods. We stand for an hour, a few people hunched over their walkers, six feet apart in the shade, waving handwritten signs at passing cars.

The evening news makes us groan and shake our fists, but Stuart and I can't help watching. As good citizens, it's the least we can do. After dinner, though, we snuggle on the couch and watch another episode of *Emily in Paris*, a glitzy romp around the city we had eagerly arranged to visit for a week in May before Covid canceled us. *Quel dommage.*

***

The Weimar Republic is teetering on the brink of collapse. Inflation has soared into hyperinflation, with prices jumping ten-fold, a hundred-fold, within hours. The cost of a single egg equals the cost of one billion eggs before the war. People go shopping with a wheelbarrow of Deutschemarks and stand in long lines to buy a loaf of bread. There are riots and looting. Communist brigades and nationalist Freikorps engage in daylong street battles in various cities. In a beer hall in Munich, Adolf Hitler, surrounded by Nazi Stormtroopers, calls on a crowd of three thousand to "begin the advance against Berlin, that Babylon of Wickedness," overthrow the government "of the November criminals," and recreate "a Germany of power and greatness. . . ." They rush out to the Defense Ministry headquarters where soldiers fire on them, killing sixteen, and the mob disperses.

"I am driving to the cabin and very much look forward to the strong mountain air," Heidegger writes Jaspers. "I don't long for the company of professors. The farmers are much more pleasant and even more interesting." The "simple folk" of the Black Forest have authenticity. "Eight days of wood-work, then writing again."

Through the handling of its projects, individual *Dasein* seeks a personal relationship to Being (*Sein*). In this quest to know the essence, however, *Dasein* is beset by anxiety. "It is already deep night," Heidegger reports. "The storm sweeps over the summits, the beams creak in the hut, life is pure, simple, and as big as the soul." Instead of experiencing authentic Being, Dasein suffers a loss of meaning, emptiness, its own possible nothingness. In a word, death. This is the existentialist moment. "With death, Dasein stands before itself in its ownmost potentiality-for-Being." We can live authentically if we choose to head resolutely toward our death.

Heidegger is working hard on his book but finds himself unexpectedly distracted. He has fallen in love with his brilliant, beautiful nineteen-year-old student Hannah Arendt, and she in turn is bowled over by her charismatic mentor. "The fact of the Other's presence breaking into our life is more than our disposition can cope with," he writes her. "I daydream about the young girl who, in a raincoat, her hat low over her quiet, large eyes, entered my office for the first time, and shortly and shyly gave a brief answer to each question. . . ." Nothing like it had ever happened to him, he exclaims. "To be in love is to be pressed into Existence."

But there is also the mundane fact that he's thirty-five years old, married with two children, so he insists they conduct their affair in secret. On the days he leaves a chalk symbol on a park bench, they meet in her attic room. When he lectures in other towns, she follows and waits for him two streetcar stops ahead. Obviously she can't work on her dissertation with him, so in the summer of 1926 she moves to Heidelberg and works with Karl Jaspers. "I will never be able to possess you," Heidegger tells her, "but you will belong in my life henceforth, and may it grow with you."

During the next two years they will continue to meet, furtively and passionately, but in retrospect Arendt's departure marks a turning point. She has chosen "The Meaning of Love in St. Augustine" as her dissertation topic. While she employs Heidegger's theoretical principles, she imitates Jaspers' approach by analyzing relationships in practice. Neighborly love, for example. Whereas Heidegger is concerned with future existence, she's concerned with past and present. Shortly after she earns her doctorate, their romantic relationship turns into a friendship.

During the summer of 1925, Heidegger writes thirty pages a day and completes his 450-page magnum opus. In *Sein und Zeit* the word *love* appears only once—in a footnote.

***

In addition to salad, Stuart arrives with her other favorite kind of project. It's a 500-piece jigsaw puzzle, a mostly white and gray winter landscape that makes my heart sink. I have fun making collages, but fitting those tiny odd-shaped pieces together makes my head hurt. Worse, there is Stuart's rule: proceed without looking at the picture on the box.

"Why must you make the task harder than it already is?" I complain.

"Why do you want to know exactly where you're going? That takes away the excitement. And a lot of the pleasure."

Stuart always avoids reading the jacket of a book. During a trailer at the movies, she closes her eyes and covers her ears. I consult reviews before deciding.

"After all," she points out, "in real life we can't know how things will turn out until they turn out."

I nod my head. No need to say aloud what we're thinking. Her husband died of a heart attack eleven years ago while running to catch a bus. Nine years ago, my thirty-year marriage expired in divorce.

She strokes my arm and recites a verse by Garth Brooks.

> Our lives are better left to chance.
> I could have missed the pain but
> I'd have had to miss the dance.

***

Fall. The virus rages out of control. Deaths spike. Trump tests positive. Three days after being hospitalized, he climbs the staircase to the White House portico, removes his mask, and raises one arm like an orange-haired Mussolini.

Biden becomes the Democratic presidential nominee.

"2020 will be the most INACCURATE & FRAUDULENT Election in history," Trump tweets his 89 million ardent followers.

In the wake of publishing his book, Heidegger has acquired a cult of admirers. At the end of every lecture, students burst into thunderous applause. In the Alpine resort of Davos, he's the star at a three-day gathering in 1929 of illustrious European philosophers. Wearing his peasant garb, Heidegger confidently debates Ernst Cassirer, the elegantly dressed, Jewish proponent of Enlightenment humanism.

But now he makes a move that leaves me bewildered and

horrified. Shortly after Hitler takes power, Heidegger agrees to be the rector of Freiburg University, which requires him to join the Nazi Party. In a hall adorned with Nazi banners, he delivers his inaugural address. "The essence of the German university," he declares, "is the will to knowledge as the will to the historical spiritual mission of the German Volk as a Volk that knows itself in its State." As for students, "You can no longer be those who merely listen to lectures." Commit yourselves "to make the sacrifices necessary to save the essence and to heighten the inner strength of our people in their State." Do not let "ideas" govern your Being (*Sein*). "The Führer himself, and he alone, is the German reality and its law today and in the future. *Heil Hitler!*"

How do we understand Heidegger's embrace of those loathsome principles? Pragmatic careerism plays a large part, as does political naivete. But he has also stepped into the trap of his own philosophical ideas. Passages in his book about "*Dasein* finding uttermost possibility in giving itself up" to the universal take on grim meaning. His fascination with authentic German culture now harmonizes with Nazi racism. Heidegger is betraying existentialism. And as the Nazis strip Jews of legal rights, he goes on to betray colleagues and friends.

At first, Jaspers is spared, but because he's married to a Jewish woman, he eventually loses his university position. With sadness, Heidegger's longtime, generous-minded friend—really his only friend—cuts off their relationship.

Arendt confronts Heidegger, but he sidesteps her questions and ducks responsibility. When she's arrested and temporarily imprisoned by the Gestapo for writing about antisemitism, she flees to Prague, Paris and finally New York. In her renowned books, she will employ Heideggerian ideas for un-Heideggerian purposes as she explains the origins of totalitarianism and endorses citizens' responsibilities in a republic. For seventeen years she will have no communication with him.

I too am done with Heidegger. My quest for lofty answers has come back to earth with a jolting lesson. *Dasein's* lonely struggle for authentic Being produced allegiance to a group of men who murdered six million human beings. I need to attend to events taking place in the world around me.

***

November. Biden wins by seven million votes.

Trump declares. "This was a RIGGED ELECTION! We won in a landslide."

January 6. "We must stop the steal," Trump tells his followers outside the White House. Many of them are wearing militia riot gear, neo-Nazi shirts, Confederate uniforms. "If you don't fight like hell, you're not going to have a country anymore. So we're going to the Capitol." Armed with baseball bats, flagpoles, hockey sticks, bear spray, and stun guns, the mob breaks into the Capitol, beats policemen, ransacks offices, chants "Hang Mike Pence," and shoots selfies.

As I watch all this on TV in my living room, I can't stop my arms from shaking. This isn't protest. It's insurrection. It's a *putsch*. For the first time in my life, I'm imagining a dictatorship in my country: Trump feeding his brutal appetite for power; the elaborate edifice of the republic crashing down upon us.

But the even more alarming fact, the chilling fact, is that most of those arrested in the Capitol don't belong to extremist groups. They're predominately middle-aged and middle-class—shop owners, accountants, IT specialists. They're ordinary men and women, representatives of the seventy-four million Americans who voted for Trump. They may be anyone, perhaps this man walking toward me in the grocery store aisle with his mask sagging on his chin.

***

The new year begins and the pandemic continues Everyone at Carol Woods has been vaccinated. Stuart and I are giddy, dancing between freedom and anxiety. Shall we go to the beach? To a movie theater? Masked or unmasked? But surely we can deliver a year's backlog of hugs to our two little granddaughters, can't we?

In any event, I'm looking forward to teaching a seminar next month here at Carol Woods: outdoors under a big tent, fifteen residents in person, unmasked. Sixty years I've been teaching, and I always feel excited and, at memorable times, authentic. My lifelong "project." I've chosen to go back to the 1920s—not to Weimar Germany, certainly not to Heidegger's hut, but to the United States. It was a decade when Americans were divided, Klan vs. immigrants; fundamentalists vs. Darwinists; "wets" vs. Prohibitionists; race riots; Red Scare. Maybe we'll gain some perspective on our own fractured era.

With romantic comedies and jigsaw puzzles, the outcome is predictable. Real life, on the other hand, acquires inevitability only when it recedes into history. Not knowing the future, we do the best we can in the meantime.

Stuart has taken ownership of her cottage and has been happily installing her belongings. This evening she will bring the makings of a salad. After dinner, we'll work together on a new jigsaw puzzle. Then we'll snuggle on the couch to watch *Love, Actually* for the umpteenth time.

[This essay was originally published online in the American Scholar, March 26, 2021.]

Personal Histories

www.ingramcontent.com/pod-product-compliance
Lightning Source LLC
Chambersburg PA
CBHW050140170426
43197CB00011B/1907